Advance

"The humanities and the arts contain powerful lessons for leaders. The practice and discipline of the performing arts and the experiential insights they bring make fertile territory for leadership development. The lessons learned can be pivotal – they stick."

Tracey Camilleri
Director Oxford Strategic Leadership Programme,
Saïd Business School, University of Oxford

"Takes us under the skin of performing artists and reveals the techniques and mindsets they use in search of a winning performance. The fictionalized approach brings everything to life and shows clearly how relevant these techniques are for all of us."

Neil Jacobsohn
FutureWorld - the Global Business & Technology Think Tank

"Goes right to the heart of what really drives business performance - the behaviours and mindsets of individuals. The innovative approach the authors take really brings to life the experiential nature of working with performing artists and draws out the lessons we can all use for our own success."

Robert Williams
Transformation Director, Denton Williams Consulting

PERFORM
TO
WIN

**UNLOCKING THE SECRETS OF THE ARTS
FOR PERSONAL AND BUSINESS SUCCESS**

Published by
LID Publishing Ltd.
One Adam Street, London. WC2N 6LE

31 West 34th St., 8th Floor, Suite 8004
New York, NY 10001, US

info@lidpublishing.com
www.lidpublishing.com

A member of:

BPR
Business Publishers Roundtable
www.businesspublishersroundtable.com

© Dr Mark Powell & Jonathan Gifford 2016
© LID Publishing Ltd. 2016

Printed in Great Britain by TJ International
ISBN: 978-1-910649-25-1

Cover and page design: Caroline Li

DR MARK POWELL &JONATHAN GIFFORD

PERFORM TO WIN

LONDON MONTERREY
MADRID SHANGHAI
MEXICO CITY BOGOTA
NEW YORK BUENOS AIRES
BARCELONA SAN FRANCISCO

DR MARK POWELL & JONATHAN GIFFORD

PERFORM TO WIN

Contents

Special thanks are due to Piers Ibbotson, previously with the Royal Shakespeare Company as both actor and assistant director, now a business consultant and senior teaching fellow at Warwick Business School at the University of Warwick, and to Peter Hanke, choral and orchestral conductor, associate fellow at Saïd Business School at the University of Oxford and associate of the Centre for Art and Leadership at Copenhagen Business School.

Piers and Peter are pioneers in their own fields of arts-based leadership development programmes. They both appear in *Perform To Win*, alongside Dr Mark Powell, co-author of the book, as the real facilitators of an imaginary development programme attended by a fictional group of board director delegates. The workshop exercises that they facilitate in the book are fictionalized, and are not presented as exact accounts of their work, but are intended to give the reader a general impression of their sophisticated workshop techniques and a broad overview of their thinking.

Piers Ibbotson is the author of *The Illusion of Leadership* (Palgrave Macmillan, 2008) ISBN 978-0-230-20199-6. Peter Hanke is the author of *Performance & Lederskab: Passionen Som Drivkraft*, (Børsens Forlag, 2008) ISBN 978-87-7664-263-1. English language extracts from this book are available under the title *Extracts From Performance & Leadership* by Peter Hanke.

Thanks are also due to the professional Latin dancers, Gunnar Gunnarsson and Marika Doshoris, who also feature as themselves in the book in a fictionalized account of a dance-based leadership development workshop.

Acknowledgements

In our previous book, *My Steam Engine Is Broken: Taking the organization from the industrial era to the age of ideas,* we argued that many organizations unthinkingly persist with a model of behaviour that has its roots in the industrial era. The rapid and hugely successful mechanization of production that started with the industrial revolution and flourished in the early twentieth century led some management thinkers to conclude that workers' abilities and outputs should be measured and managed in exactly the same way as the machines that were revolutionizing global industry. In this mindset, people should be seen as a resource like any other, to be used as 'efficiently' as possible, and their behaviour should be tightly governed and controlled.

This mechanistic view of the organization is no longer fit for purpose in the knowledge economy, which needs people's uniquely human skills: their emotional intelligence, their creativity and their ability to form distinctive communities that are far more than mere collections of individuals. The inappropriate persistence of old-fashioned organizational behaviours leads to the chronic and damaging employee disengagement that is of such concern in the modern workplace. There is a growing gap between what people want and expect from their places of work, and what they actually experience day to day. This disconnect plays out in lost ideas and wasted energy.

The lack of commitment and engagement of people in the typical workplace stands in sharp contrast to the ways in which people behave in other contexts: people are increasingly turning to other activities to supply the passion and fulfilment that their place of work fails to provide. In these contexts, people's energies are once again released as they commit themselves fully to something that they care about and have willingly committed to.

This is especially true of the performing arts. People who choose to come together to 'put on a show' don't do this half-heartedly. It is not possible to be disengaged from a successful performance; there is a direct link between the energy of the performers and their performance.

Introduction

There is also a direct link between every individual perfor-mance and the performance of the other artists involved. A great theatrical performance is dependent on the support of the entire ensemble; two dance partners perform brilliantly togethe to deliver a winning performance or they fail; an orchestra o choir only succeed when every singer or musician performs thei part exceptionally.

There is a growing recognition in the business world that the performing arts have much to offer as a model for more successfu organizational behaviours (or 'performances'), but it is difficult tc bridge the gap between these two very different worlds. The thing that performing artists do and the ways in which they think are hard to put into words; these are things that ideally need to be experienced and felt at a visceral level to acquire their full meaning

This book aims to bridge the gap between the vibrant, 3D worlc of the performing arts and the equally vibrant world of business by using a narrative form – by bringing the story to life. *Perform To Win* portrays a fictionalized group of board directors facing a very real business problem and follows them through a three-da arts-based programme, during which they explore the mindset and practices of performing artists by observing and working with artists at a very close and intimate level. The activities they take part in and the experiences they share are based entirely on rea activities and experiences, and the outcomes are based entirely or real outcomes: people who experience arts-based programme emerge with new perspectives, new energies and new ways o working with their colleagues. They also find that their new way of thinking have benefits in their personal lives. The focus, energ and skill that great performing artists bring to their work, anc the ways in which they form a deep connection with their fellov performers in search of a winning performance, offer a model for success in every kind of human activity.

Perform to Win

Perform to Win explores the mindset, attitudes and techniques used by performing artists to deliver winning performances, and sets out the ten most significant things that great performing artists do differently from the rest of us; ten core lessons from which we can learn, to help us deliver winning performances in our personal and business lives.

The book is based on Dr Mark Powell's years of experience in designing and running leadership development programmes. Over these years, Dr Powell's programmes have made increasing use of arts-based sessions, offering executives experiences that can help to deliver new perspectives and potential new approaches to the challenges that they face: sessions with poets and painters; actors and conductors; jazz musicians and storytellers. His work convinces him that it is experiencing something in a physical sense that allows delegates to gain the most meaningful new realizations: a new way of thinking; a new approach; a different mindset that allows them to see things with fresh eyes.

As Dr Powell told Jonathan Gifford, co-author of this book, in a recent conversation:

"Having spent so many years with so many people on leadership programmes, there is no question in my mind that the things that really stick with people have two things in common. One is that they are experiential; people experience things in a way that hits them as a human being in some way – it doesn't matter what it is. And those things tend to be arts-based, by definition. The second thing is that people are more open to learning if they are presented with something in a context that they are not familiar with. If you ask people to learn from something in an area that they are expert in, they generally close down to learning, at least to some extent. So to make an impact – to change the way that people think and behave – what works best, in my experience, is something that people can witness and feel in an immediate way, in a context that is out of their normal realm of experience. That's why arts-based learning is so effective. It presents something that is dramatic, but also entirely human, entirely understandable at a gut level. Something in an arts-based programme will hit everyone at a visceral level. It won't be the same thing; people react differently. But there will be something that hits them at an instinctive level and makes them just 'get it'. And when they have experienced that, it really sticks. That's not something they know today but forget tomorrow. That's now a part of their makeup. And it's very powerful."

The fact that we learn many things though experience, at a pre-rational level, is easy to forget. We have come to see ourselves first and foremost as creatures of reason, and we forget how much of our understanding of the world – and of other people, in particular – is embodied. We acquire this knowledge through our senses, not through our rational minds, and it works within us at a pre-conscious, pre-rational level.

In the field of psychology, there is a famous case that demonstrates this compellingly.

Henry Molaison was born in 1926, in Connecticut, US. As he grew up, he experienced increasingly serious epileptic fits. Molaison's epileptic episodes became so severe that, in 1953, it was decided to operate on his brain. It was believed at the time – perhaps 'hoped' is more accurate – that removing parts of his brain would reduce the levels of brain activity associated with epileptic fits: most of Molaison's hippocampus and amygdala were removed. This did, in fact, cure Molaison's epilepsy, but also destroyed his ability to form new memories. He could remember almost nothing from the year or so before his operation, though he could remember some things before that time, but he could not form new memories of things that happened to him after the operation; he was completely amnesiac.

Because Molaison could remember some things, we know that memory itself is not located in the parts of the brain that were removed. Memory is either stored somewhere else or more diffusely. But neuroscientists could be absolutely sure that the regions of the brain that were removed or damaged in Molaison's case are essential, in some way, to the process of forming new memories.

But researchers found, to their great surprise, that although Molaison could not form new memories, he could learn new skills. He was taught to trace the shape of a five-pointed star by looking at the reflection of the star and his hand in a mirror. This is surprisingly difficult. Everything is backwards; you have to train the hand tracing the shape to do the opposite of what it instinctively does.

Molaison learned how to do this, and he got better at it – but had no memory of having learned the skill. Whenever he was given the task, it seemed to him that he had never seen it before, though, in fact, he was getting better at it all the time.

Learning 'how to do' something is an entirely different process from remembering facts and figures, and has nothing to do with the parts of the brain that are responsible for forming new memories. Molaison couldn't remember new facts or events, but he could acquire new physical skills. Despite his shaky memory of facts and events from the past, Molaison also retained his social skills: he was pleasant, even amusing, company, even though he would have no idea whether his companion was a stranger or an old friend.

Large parts of our behaviour have nothing to do with 'what we know' and can 'remember'. We readily acknowledge that our level of emotional intelligence is a key factor in determining how successful we can be in most areas of life but we act as if we can acquire emotional intelligence by reading about it, or by attending lectures. In reality, this kind of embodied knowledge is acquired through experience and can only be enhanced by experience.

This is the realm of the arts. We use the arts to explore the human condition, and have done for millennia. We all understand artistic expression in exactly the same way that we understand facial expression, the nuances of the human voice and body language; expertise in human behaviour is something we acquire, for free, as we grow up in the world. Most of us have our favourite art forms, and these enrich us by enhancing, and even changing, the way in which we experience the world; by giving us insights into aspects of human behaviour. It should come as no surprise that what we can learn from the arts can enhance our experience of the world of work, just as it enhances our private lives.

∗ ∗ ∗

Learning facts and acquiring knowledge-based skills is a mental process. Learning things that will actually change our behaviour is far more likely to come through bodily experience.

In this book, we follow a fictional board of directors as they experience an imagined three-day, arts-based workshop at a UK business school. The sessions they attend are based on those facilitated by real people, who feature in this narrative as themselves: Dr Mark Powell, co-author of this book, ex-champion ballroom dancer, management consultant and associate fellow at Saïd Business School at the University of Oxford; Piers Ibbotson, ex-Royal Shakespeare Company actor and assistant director, now a business consultant and senior teaching fellow at Warwick Business School at the University of Warwick; and Peter Hanke, choral and orchestral conductor, associate fellow at Saïd Business School at the University of Oxford and associate of the Centre for Art and Leadership at Copenhagen Business School.

What the facilitators say and do in the book is based on the sessions that they run in real life and on material drawn from their writings, but is not an actual transcript of real sessions or a precise description of real exercises. The workshops as described in the book should be seen as fictional accounts that offer an accurate reflection of the kinds of experiences that executives attending arts-based development programmes would undergo, rather than as an exact account of real development sessions.

As our fictional characters progress through the programme, we hope you will share in these experiences and get an understanding of their various realizations and 'aha!' moments as the delegates explore how performing artists work together to deliver great performances. We have also set out some off the difficulties and frustrations experienced by the delegates as they work through the programme. Arts-based programmes are very different from programmes that deliver new skill sets, theories and best practices; they set out instead to offer delegates new perspectives and changed behaviours. It is impossible to predict how any individual will interact with any programme or what will give them the most profound insight but, in Dr Powell's long experience of such programmes, there is always something that offers a new perspective and opens the way to improved performance. At the start of the book, we give our fictional board members a very real business problem, and set out to show how their experiences as they progress through the programme help them to see their problem in a new light and to find new ways of working together towards a solution.

The core ideas about performance that emerge throughout the book are summarized at the end of each chapter. The final chapter explores what we believe are the ten most significant things that great performing artists do in order to deliver winning performances. At their heart is the understanding that the performance of every member of an ensemble is vital to the overall effect, and that ensembles succeed together, or not at all.

The Worst
Moment

Jack Isherwood put down the phone and stared blankly at his desk. He got to his feet with a rising sense of panic and looked around the office as if searching for an escape. He started to feel physically sick. He forced himself to breathe slowly and took a sip of water. Isherwood was the CEO of a successful engineering company based in Bedfordshire, England, and he had just finished the worst phone call of his career.

One week after his colleagues made a competitive pitch to renew their long-standing contract with a major car manufacturer, Isherwood's assistant put through the call from the manufacturer's purchasing director, Michael Browning. Isherwood was surprised to receive a call from the purchasing director himself – usually one of Browning's managers gave the good news to Isherwood's sales director, and the sales director and the purchasing manager would see to the renewal of the contract.

Isherwood took the call with a bad feeling that they were going to be asked to renegotiate costs, though price itself had never been a major issue in the past. Maybe they could adjust the overall package to reach an agreement. The conversation did not go the way he had expected.

"Good morning Jack," said the purchasing director. "I wanted to have this conversation with you myself, because our companies have a long history and you are one of our most valued suppliers."

"Thank you Michael."

"First, I want to thank you and the team for your pitch. You obviously put a lot of work into it, as ever, and it was a thorough job."

"Our pleasure."

"Jack, I have to tell you that we don't intend to renew our contract with you."

Isherwood didn't manage to say anything before Browning filled the increasingly awkward gap.

"We saw some very exciting competitive pitches and feel it's time to make a change," said Browning.

Isherwood managed to regain his voice.

"Um, when you say 'exciting' Michael, what do you mean? We

think our prices are very reasonable, considering the service level agreements that…"

Browning quickly cut in. "Jack, this is not about price. If it were, we would do you the courtesy of having another conversation with you."

Browning seemed to struggle to find the right words; he sounded embarrassed.

"Jack, our companies go back a long way and, funnily enough, we can't really fault you. You deliver what you promise and you've never let us down. It's just that …" He trailed off, but jumped in again before Isherwood could say anything. "Jack, the other presentations were just what I said they were: they were exciting. We got the feeling that one of your competitors, in particular, was full of good ideas. We felt they were challenging us to think differently. We pride ourselves on being at the cutting edge, Jack."

Isherwood started to mumble some form of praise and agreement, but Browning was in full flow.

"It's a tough market, and it's not getting easier. You know that, Jack. If we're not producing new, innovative stuff, then whatever we're putting out starts to get commoditized the minute it hits the market. So we have to keep innovating and we need all the help we can get: we need our suppliers to surprise us. We need them to help give us new ideas. Our relationship with your company is fine: we give you a specification, you give us a price and you deliver. That's great. But that's all that happens. Your team came in to present to us and they didn't tell us anything we didn't know already. They told us we'd asked for this, that and the other and then they told us that you had delivered this, that and the other. We know that. Then they told us that you could keep delivering stuff for another three years at a marginally increased cost. That's not news, Jack. That's not exciting.'

He stopped, suddenly.

"I'm sorry Jack, I've said too much. You guys are great. I'm just trying to explain why we feel it's time for a change. Being reliable is nice, but it's not exceptional. We need 'exceptional' right now."

Part of Isherwood's mind was watching his company unravel as he waved goodbye to the key account that underpinned its finances; another part was listening intently to every inflection of Browning's voice.

"Please don't apologize, Michael. Thank you for sharing this with me. You could have just told me that you've gone with another bid. I appreciate it. At this stage, I only have one question: do we have another chance? Can we talk to your guys, really try to get our heads around what you need, and come back with another pitch? I know it's asking a lot."

"Well, Jack, you know – you've made your pitch. It's a bit weird to let you do another pitch because the first pitch didn't work."

"I understand that, Michael, but, as you said, we have a lot of history between our companies. I don't mean that in any kind of 'you owe us' sense; I just mean that there's a lot of good stuff that could be lost if you move away from us now. I mean, the other guys can promise anything, but they may not deliver, you know? It's a big gamble. I hear what you're saying, and it's obvious that we have to raise our game. I'm up for that, personally. We have a six-month work-out on our contract, right? If we can get back to you again in a month, does that give you time to think about this one last time?"

Browning was quiet. Isherwood waited.

"The other guys will need at least six months to tool up if we give them the contract," said Browning finally. "It's a big decision for us and a big step up for them. We might need you to cover our backs while we make the changeover. We can't rush this. And you're right, there are possible downsides. But we're not asking anything simple from you here, Jack, we're asking you to be different – you know, to think differently; to behave differently. That's a big ask. Why would that even be possible?"

"That's a good question, Michael," said Isherwood. "But what you're telling me is that if we don't change, we've lost our most important contract. You know how important your business is to us. I'm not going to pretend it isn't. So I'm up for change, Michael. Can you give us one month and the chance of another conversation?"

There was a pause. Isherwood tried not to breathe.

"We owe you that much. You've done a lot for us. But you're coming from behind now. A lot of people are beginning to imagine a new future with new partners. You're going to need to come in with something pretty spectacular."

Isherwood breathed out. "Thank you Michael," he said. "I think we can do that."

"Well – you're welcome, Jack. But it's a tall order. You're going to need to come in with a team of people who behave and think very differently from the team we saw last month."

"Uh, yes. Wish us luck."

"Good luck!"

Isherwood was still staring blankly at his office walls when his assistant came in.

"How was Mr Browning?" she asked.

Isherwood had regained some of his composure.

"Not good, Janet, not good. Please ask the board to come to an extraordinary meeting tomorrow morning at 8am. Let's have some kind of breakfast on offer – pastries or something."

* * *

The following morning, a subdued board met in the company's head office, an unglamorous three-storey block next to the manufacturing facility on an industrial estate near the town of Luton, England. The double glazing dulled the constant buzz of traffic from the nearby ring road, but the roar of planes taking off from the nearby airport occasionally interrupted the conversation.

Jack Isherwood looked at the uneasy faces of his top team and broke the news about the failure of the pitch.

"I don't need to tell you about the potential consequences of this," he told them. "Without this account, we have to restructure completely. I think we can stay in business, but on a completely different footing. We have nearly 1,000 employees now, here and at the plant in Scotland. That would be completely unsustainable."

He turned to his finance director, Andrew Gibbon. "Andrew, I need you and your team to draw up a set of figures for the worst-case scenario, if you would – as soon as possible. Thank you."

"Can I ask, Jack – what did Browning say?" asked Roger Corbett, the sales director. "The pitch went well. Everyone seemed happy. All our usual guys at the client seem fine."

"He said that we weren't exciting enough, and that one of our competitors had come up with a lot of new ideas. He said they needed ideas from their suppliers to help them stay in front."

"What sort of ideas?" asked Roger.

"If I knew that, we wouldn't be having this meeting," said Isherwood.

"I don't see how we can drop our prices significantly and still deliver what they expect," said Andrew Gibbon, the finance director.

"Well, to keep the account it might be worth reducing our charges," said John Winters, the chief operating officer. "It's not ideal, but we could shave some areas to bring costs down."

"I really believe that this is not about price," said Isherwood. "If it were, Michael would have come straight out with it. He sounded embarrassed. He kept saying he couldn't really fault us but that we hadn't offered them anything new: we just told them what they already knew – that we were hitting our targets."

Roger suddenly felt the need to defend the presentation they had delivered at the pitch.

"We all signed off on the presentation," he said firmly. "It was very impressive. We hit every single target we were given. Delivery, quality control, everything. We tooled up successfully for their new product line, and that went smoothly. All the people I talk to at the client are happy. Where is this coming from?"

"Did Michael give you any idea about who was driving this?" asked Margaret Simons, the company's human resources director.

"No, he sounded pretty involved. It sounded as if he wasn't just giving somebody else's opinion. But it probably goes further than him."

"When they say that they want new ideas, do they mean new

technical solutions?" asked Rory Campbell, the chief technical officer. "We'd need a lot more input from them before we could propose anything."

"He said they wanted to be 'surprised', said Isherwood. "I honestly don't know if they have any particular problem that needs solving. Roger?" He looked at the sales director.

"If there was something new in the wind that affected us, we'd be the first to know about it," said Roger.

"So we need to surprise them," said Rory, "but they can't tell us what sort of surprise they would like?"

"I guess that's the joy of surprises," said Isherwood, drily. "Look. Gentlemen, Margaret. If we lose this account hundreds of jobs will go. I'm not even sure whether the company that would emerge after the shakedown would be viable in the long term. This is potentially a matter of life or death. This company is 80 years old and I have been CEO for nearly a quarter of its lifespan. I am damned if it is going to go under on my watch. I'm sure you all feel the same.

"I have bought us some time, to give it one last go. We get to go back in with a new presentation and it needs to be pretty spectacular. Michael said that he would need to see what he called 'a very different team.'"

The team shuffled slightly in their chairs and Isherwood realized the possible meaning of what he had just said.

"There is no suggestion that they have a problem with any of us individually," Isherwood reassured them. "But it's clear that, at the moment, we don't have the right attitude. We're not sending out the right messages. We're not impressing them. Maybe they do need to see some new faces."

"How long have we got?" asked Roger.

"One month. Maybe we can stretch that a bit by the time they find us a diary slot, but we shouldn't bank on that."

Roger leaned back in his chair, looked up at the ceiling and let his hands drop into his lap, rather dramatically.

"You don't think we can do it, Roger?" Isherwood asked pointedly.

"It took us two months to put together the last pitch. I don't see how we can put a new presentation together in less. And I have no idea what we are going to say that is any different."

"All I can tell you is that it has to be something different," said Isherwood. "Throw away the old presentation. What else can we do for the client in the next three years other than hit the targets they set us? We need to rethink our pitch from top to bottom. Has anyone got any ideas?"

Margaret raised her hand.

"Margaret?"

"We're all due to attend a new leadership development programme next week; an arts-based programme. I'm hopeful it will give us some new perspectives. We could use the time to think about the proposal. I'm sure the teaching staff will be helpful – it will give them a real, practical focus to work on. And we'll be together, away from the office. I think we may gain some insights that will steer us in the right direction."

"Jack, forgive me," broke in Rory, "but if this is Margaret's pet 'dancing with ballerinas' project …"

"It is not 'dancing with ballerinas' Rory, as you know perfectly well," Margaret broke in, sharply. "It's an arts-based leadership development programme at a leading business school, led by a leading business consultant. It happens to involve musicians and actors and dancers and conductors. It's designed to challenge our thinking and make us more effective leaders. It's about helping us to work better as a team."

"Frankly, I think it should be cancelled while we deal with this problem," replied Rory. "I personally think it's a waste of time and money anyway – but right now we clearly haven't got the time to spare. There must be something Browning isn't telling us: some technical problem. If we can find out what it is, we can come up with a fix. Spending three days listening to jazz or conducting choirs or whatever Margaret has got planned is not going to help."

"I don't believe that there is any one 'problem', Rory, and I don't think there's any one 'fix'," said Isherwood. "I think this is about our attitude, our ideas and our relationship with the client. I think we need to be offering some innovative solutions. I don't know what they are. I wish I did. But we need to put on our thinking caps and come up with something to make the client feel we are the right partner for them for the rest of the 21st century. We need to be exciting and I don't think that we are very exciting right now." Isherwood stared out of the window at the nearby elevated ring road, now filled with slow-moving traffic. The sky was overcast and a light rain had begun to spot the windows.

"This programme is highly recommended," said Margaret. "It's all about changing mindsets and attitudes by tapping into the way performing artists work together to produce exceptional outcomes. I think it's just what we need, Jack. It could help us to come up with those new ideas."

"Do we really have the time?" asked Roger. "We have to come up with a new proposal and create a new presentation. That's weeks of work."

"We need the ideas first, then we'll make the time to create the presentation. Maybe we don't sleep much for a week or three. I can live with that," said Margaret.

"This is a big risk, Jack," said Roger. "Nearly a week out of the office doing wacky stuff when we have a real crisis. I say we hunker down here and do nothing but work on the presentation for the next month."

"Andrew, what do you think?" asked Isherwood, turning to his finance director.

"I've got my hands full doing the scenarios Jack. I'm assuming I won't be asked to go, but in any case my advice would also be to postpone it. I'm guessing they'll hit us with a cancellation fee, but saving the account outweighs that cost."

"John?" asked Isherwood, turning to his COO. "You haven't said much today?"

"Thanks Jack," said Winters. "I agree with Roger that it's a risk taking time out when we could be working on the re-pitch, but then, as Margaret says, we get to tap into the brains at the business school. I've looked at the programme materials Margaret sent us and it looks fascinating. That seems to be what we need right now, three days of 'thinking outside of the box'. The five of us will be together, away from the office. It will be a great opportunity to get our heads together and rethink our whole approach. Hopefully we'll come back with new ideas. I think we should go ahead."

Isherwood leant forward, his elbows on the boardroom table and his hands over his lower face. He looked around at his colleagues; after a pause, he drew his hands down, clasped them together in front of him and sat back.

"I don't do this very often, but I'm going to make a little speech. I'm going to be completely honest with you. That phone call yesterday was the worst moment of my time with his company. In some ways, it was the worst moment of my life. I've been lucky enough not to suffer any major personal tragedies, and this company means a great deal to me. I don't mind sharing with you that I felt scared and I felt stupid. That account has become far too important to us, and we've got complacent. Our contract has been renewed at every review during the 15 years we've had the business. None of us imagined we might lose the account – but losing it is potentially fatal to us. How stupid is that?"

He looked around the table. Most of his colleagues' eyes were fixed on his. Some were looking down at their hands.

"Our competitors are being smarter than we are in some way, and we don't even know what that means. They are 'surprising' our client. Browning obviously feels they would be more exciting to work with, and I guess he believes business would go better as a result. Nobody wants excitement for excitement's sake. But I don't think that this is about some new invention. Forgive me, Rory," he said, nodding at his chief technical officer, "I don't believe that our competition has come up with some brilliant new widget. If they had, Michael would have said, 'These guys are developing this amazing technology and they've got two years' lead on you on it' … or something."

He looked around the room.

"It can't be about that; it must about new ideas in the broadest sense. It must be about ways of working together."

Isherwood stopped suddenly, as if he had made up his mind about something.

"That's exactly what it is," he said, looking up at his colleagues. "Browning said that his colleagues were already imagining a future working with these new partners, and that was clearly a more exciting future. He said that if we went in again, we would need to be 'a changed team.' He's not talking about skills and capabilities, or new widgets, he's talking about attitudes and relationships; things that may lead to new and better widgets in the future. Our competitors have said and done something that has made him think working with them would be better; more fruitful.

"Here's what I would like you to do. I would like you all to go on the programme next week. Margaret, thank you for sourcing it. I looked at what the programme was offering and it seems very interesting; very challenging. It might give us new ways of seeing things. I've been thinking for some time that we need to shake ourselves up." He stopped, with a rueful half smile. "Obviously, I was too slow.

"So you will go on this programme – you too, Andrew. Finance is critical to this; I don't want people thinking that finance just crunches the numbers after the event; we need your creative input. Your team can start to run the numbers while you're away. Don't let them ring you every five minutes during the programme either. I don't want you to be distracted. I want you all to go and dance with these bloody ballerinas..." There were more smiles, and Margaret was about to begin another protest when Isherwood stopped her with a gesture, smiling.

"I'm just being facetious, Margaret. I want you all to go and do whatever the boffins tell you to do and I want you to be open to this. I want you to think about how we could do things differently. Anything. Everything."

Isherwood stood up and looked at his colleagues for a few seconds. He moved away from his chair, took a few thoughtful steps, turned around and sat back down.

"We are a team," he said finally. "I think we're a good team. We are facing a problem at the moment that I don't have an answer to. I don't think any of us does. But I believe that, together, and I mean in terms of the whole company, we can get through this. We need to reach out to everybody in the company and ask for their help. We need to talk to everybody we know at the client and listen very hard to what they have to say.

"I want you all to go on this development programme and be open to every idea that is presented to you and to pick every brain that you meet and then to come back and start work on the re-pitch. All of you, together. I will do whatever I can to help. I don't know the answer to this problem, so there's no point in me trying to dictate anything. I want you to surprise me, and then I want you to surprise the client.

"While you're away, I'll walk the floors and let people know there's still someone in charge around here. That won't do me any harm – perhaps I'll learn something useful! Thank you gentlemen; Margaret. We have to win this one back. Good luck!"

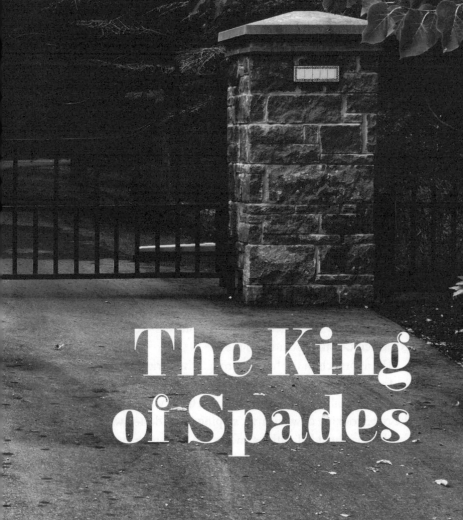

The King
of Spades

The five board members started their three-day programme on Monday morning, arriving in a chauffeured people carrier. The journey had taken not much more than an hour once the last person had been collected, with one slow patch of rush hour traffic.

It was a fine day. As their journey took them west, the countryside became more rural. Everyone was quiet. None of the board had been at the company for long enough to experience life without their main account. It had been the mainstay of their business. Jobs would have to be shed; it would be foolish to imagine that even their own roles were necessarily secure. It was possible to imagine the company surviving in a much slimmed-down form, but difficult to imagine a way forward. None of the old economies of scale would work in their favour anymore; they would go from being a relatively large enterprise to a fairly small one. It would take at least a year to pitch for, win, and tool up for another major contract; probably longer. Their other clients were far smaller than the main account, and each was very different from the other. Overnight, they would become a kind of boutique engineering company supplying different business niches. It was a whole new world, and a daunting prospect.

The car pulled into a long driveway through tall ironwork gates. The business school was set in rolling parkland set with magnificent mature trees: oak; beech; cedar; horse-chestnut; yew. There had been a great house on this site since the sixteenth century and the current estate was the remnant of the deer park that had surrounded it. The original building had been replaced in the nineteenth-century by a large neo-classical country house, much extended when it was acquired by the business school, to provide extra facilities and accommodation.

The approach to the house through the parkland was stunning. As the white stuccoed frontage came into view, with its classical portico and tall sash-framed windows, there was a brief glimpse of the river, looking down a large, sloping lawn, dotted with trees and shrubs and threaded with pathways. They were greeted warmly at reception, given welcome packs and shown to their rooms.

The group reassembled for coffee and pastries and were introduced to the programme facilitator, Dr Mark Powell. They chatted over coffee until Mark ushered them into a conference room. The room was relatively small, to suit their small group, with a screen at one end. A projector suspended from the ceiling threw an image of the business school's logo onto the screen, together with a welcome message.

The six people sat around an oval table.

"Thank you," said Mark. "We've all been introduced, but if I may, I'd like to go round the table and ask you to tell me two interesting facts about yourself, interesting things you've done in the past, one of which your colleagues may know already and, ideally, one they will not know! The interesting things should be nothing to do with your career and I would be especially interested if any of them have to do with being involved in any kind of performance. I think being second shepherd in the nativity play at primary school probably doesn't count, but apart from that..."

The team laughed and Mark turned to the person on his left.

"Rory, hard luck! You get to go first!"

Rory was middle-aged, like all of his colleagues. He had a distinct, but not broad, Scottish accent. He was slightly built and wiry and his hair and beard had a reddish tint. It would, in fact, have been hard to imagine that Rory was anything other than Scottish. He looked as if he wished he were somewhere else.

"Well, I'm an engineer, you know?" said Rory, smiling thinly. "Engineers don't do anything interesting. But I'll give it a go. One interesting fact about me that my colleagues probably do know is that I'm a 'Munro bagger.' My wife and I, and sometimes the kids now that they're old enough, like to climb the Munro peaks in Scotland whenever we get the chance – Munros are mountains over 3,000 feet, and I've personally bagged over 100 now. There's reckoned to be 282 Munros, so I don't know if my legs are going to last long enough to get up them all! The other interesting thing about me that I don't think the team know is that I used to play the bass guitar in a band when I was at university in Aberdeen.

I don't know what kind of music you would call it now, but it
was very loud. I made sure we had a very big sound system!"
Rory seemed to cheer up slightly as he remembered his days
playing music.

"What was the band called?" asked Mark.

"We were actually called 'Hammered'. We thought that was funny."

"It is funny!" agreed Mark. He turned to John Winters, the chief
operating officer, who was sitting next to Rory.

"John?"

Winters still had a fair amount of black hair, greying at the
temples and a little thin on top. His fine features and strong chin
retained some of his youthful good looks.

"Two interesting facts!" he said, smiling slightly. "That's hard.
Well, I used to be a keen sailor – dinghy sailing on reservoirs and
lakes. I started at university, and went on to compete at club level,
and I still do it for fun when I get the chance. We still have a boat
at a local lake. I haven't done a lot of performing – not since my
school days – but I used to play in the band for our school musicals.
Clarinet and saxophone. I started off in the school orchestra, and
we had a great music teacher who used to organize really quite professional school musicals. So I think the highlight of my performing career is probably our sixth-form production of *South Pacific*,
which if I may say so, was a damned fine show!"

"Thank you, John," said Mark. "Margaret?"

Margaret Simons was in her early fifties, smartly dressed, with
neatly styled blond hair and a ready smile.

"One interesting fact about me that I'm pretty sure my colleagues don't know is that I once appeared on *Top Of The Pops* –
in the audience, obviously! – when I was a teenager. And I'm not
going to tell you what year it was, but Kate Bush was on, singing
'Wuthering Heights'! In terms of performing, my guilty secret is
that I did a lot of dancing at university and for a while afterwards.
I took salsa classes at uni and I just loved it. So I kept up the classes
for a bit afterwards, but never entered any competitions. I really
wasn't any good!"

"Excellent," said Mark. "I will tell you my own interesting facts in a moment. Roger?"

He turned to Roger Corbett.

Roger was very tall and heavily built, with thinning hair and a neatly trimmed beard. Both beard and hair were now turning quite grey.

"I think my colleagues know this interesting fact about me, which is that I was in the Royal Marine Reserve for many years when I was younger. I did the whole commando training thing and got my green beret. I was a lot fitter then. And a lot thinner!" Roger made a deprecatory gesture towards his waistline.

"Roger could kill us all with his bare hands if he wanted to," joked John.

"Nonsense!" said Roger, looking secretly flattered.

"On the performance side," he continued, "I think I can surprise my colleagues. I was a choirboy at our church for many years. My dad was a lay reader and suggested I join the choir when I was about ten. It was a good choir. Practice every Wednesday and Friday. Matins and Evensong every Sunday. Weddings, if you were lucky, on Saturdays, which we got paid for. I got to be head choirboy, and wore a lovely ruffle and a cassock and a white surplice with a red pendant around my neck. I had a good treble voice and used to sing the solo verse of 'Once in Royal David's City' every Christmas. But when my voice broke it never seemed to settle. I couldn't work out if I was a tenor or a bass and I dropped out of the choir and haven't sung since." Roger suddenly looked wistful.

"I can just picture you in your ruffle and surplice," said Margaret. "You must have looked so sweet!"

"Yes, thank you Margaret," said Roger, gruffly.

"Marvelous!" said Mark. "Thank you." He turned to the final member of the group. Andrew Gibbon was tall, though not quite as tall as Roger, and slimly built. He had neatly trimmed dark hair above his ears and at the back of his neck but the top of his head was quite bald. He wore heavy-rimmed spectacles and looked rather studious.

"It's a moderately interesting fact about me that I used to do quite a lot of motocross when I was at school: you know, off-road motorcycle racing. We did compete as clubs, and I've got a few trophies, but it was really just for fun. My dad used to ride a motorcycle, so he was very supportive, but my mother was not keen. Then I broke my foot in a bit of a crash and that was the end of that! And in terms of performance, I can reveal…" He looked around at his colleagues with something of a twinkle in his eye, "that I was a leading member of the dramatic society at university. And my performance as Algernon in our *Importance of Being Earnest* was widely acclaimed. Well, some people said it was quite good." He smiled a rare, rather bashful smile. "I did keep up with a bit of amateur dramatics for a while, but it became hard to find the time."

"Thank you," said Mark. "Now, let me reveal my own interesting facts.

"The first is that I had a brief and spectacularly unsuccessful career as a racing driver! The second is that I have twice won the world Latin ballroom dancing championship. To be more precise, I have won the English, UK and British (twice) and the World (twice) over-35 Latin dance championships. When I was a student I won the British and International student Latin championship."

The team looked suitably surprised and impressed.

"I started dancing when I was a student at Cambridge and got hooked," Mark continued. "I got my PhD from Cambridge Judge Business School, and went to work in consultancy, but kept dancing as an amateur. I've been dancing competitively for over 20 years, and a business consultant for all of that time and more, so I know a lot about business and I know a lot about working on a performance until it is a winning performance. There is a lot about the mindset and techniques of performing artists that is very different from how business people tend to think.

"The performing arts offer a direct link between performance and energy; you take your energy and make a performance out of it, because you are your performance. It's very direct. It's what you do in the moment, and you get feedback immediately in the sense of that worked, or that didn't work, and also, crucially, whether the audience liked it or not."

Mark looked around, Margaret looked attentive. Everyone else looked a little distracted.

"In my experience," Mark continued, "when things go wrong in business, it's because there's a disconnect between energy and performance. It's very rarely a technical issue that can be fixed. That would be easy. Either the energy isn't there in the first place, or more likely, it's misdirected or frustrated. And the best way to explore a disconnect between energy and performance is via the arts. I believe that if we could translate even 5% of how the arts achieve performance into the business context, that would deliver a huge result."

John Winters looked as if he was becoming a little more interested.

"So that's what we're going to look at over the next three days. What is it that performing artists do to create a winning performance, and what can we take away from that and successfully apply to the world of business?

"I'd like to introduce a few of the key concepts we're going to talk about in the next few days, and they all revolve around the fundamental concept of performance. In the case of your company, we're going to talk about your organizational performance, in the broadest sense. In the case of performing artists who you're going to meet in the next few days, we're going to talk about their individual performances – what they do to create an outstanding, winning performance, and, more importantly, their performance as a partnership or as a group or ensemble. We're not going to talk about artists who work entirely on their own. Painters, sculptors, writers, poets, that kind of thing. We could talk about them, and in fact we do work with painters and poets and so on in other sessions, and it is absolutely fascinating, but that's not what we're going to do this week.

"One thing about me that I'll give you for free is that I'm very competitive and when I was dancing, I was dancing to win. I didn't want to be kind of ok at it and have some fun, I wanted to be the best and I wanted to win prizes, which I did. The thing with dancing is that it's a lot like sport, in that you can just get together and kick a ball around the park, or you can join a team and suddenly you're in a league; you're in a competition, and you want to win. And you start to want very much to win!"

Mark looked around the table, hands and eyebrows raised, with a kind of 'is that so wrong?' gesture. People smiled. Roger looked especially happy. 'Winning' was the kind of language he could relate to. He wondered how Mark was going to get from useful concepts such as winning to entirely useless concepts such as dancing and playing music.

"The thing that I worked out very early when I was dancing," Mark continued, "was that I could be absolutely brilliant; I could deliver a wonderful performance – but if my partner was not also delivering a brilliant performance, I wouldn't win. There was no way the judges were going to choose us. It also doesn't work if I'm brilliant and she's brilliant but we don't look good together. You win *as a partnership*, or you don't win. Simple as that. And that means a lot of things.

"One fundamental point we're going to be talking about this week is that you have to enable your partner or your fellow players; you have to do whatever they need in order for them to deliver their own winning performance. You have to be brilliant yourself, but if you're not there for your partner, in the moment, responding to them and delivering whatever they need so that they can be brilliant too – you're stuffed.

"I'm going to argue that performing artists have a different mindset from most people. Certainly from most business people. Actually, I'm not going to 'argue' that, it's just true. I've been a competitive dancer, a businessman and a business consultant, and I know this is true. I know what performing artists do that enables winning performances – the way they think; the way they interact with their fellow performers. And that's what we're going to share with you.

"In my experience, however, if we give you a series of Power-Point presentations about what performing artists do, nothing will change. You might well understand it, at an intellectual level, but it wouldn't make any difference. It wouldn't change anything that you do, any of your behaviours: you would not actually 'get it' at a visceral level; at a gut level. It's exactly like riding a bike: I can give you an explanation of how to ride a bike, but if you've never ridden a bike you will fall off. You don't 'know' how to ride a bike until your body knows how to ride a bike."

There was some general nodding and smiling.

"So, we're going to try to give you some new experiences, give you some new insights; some new, 'Ah, I get that now!' moments. I would suggest that all of you probably have most of the skills that you need to do your jobs very well," Mark continued, looking around the group, who made self-deprecating gestures.

"I mean, there's always something else to learn, but – at your level – what will help you to be more effective in your role is not some new skill, or new set of facts, it's finding a new way of see- ing things and a new way of relating to the people that you deal with. Because it's all about people. If it was just about processes, we could automate everything. I mean everything. Some people seem to think you can do that – replace human decision making with algorithms. Good luck to them. You can automate a mechanical process, but when people are involved, you need other people.

"So we're hoping to bring you some new 'aha!' moments. Some 'oh, I see!' moments. And we're going to try to do that by taking you through various experiences. Because I can tell you, 'this is how dancers grasp instinctively what their partner wants to do next,' or, 'this is how conductors help their choirs make wonderful music,' or 'this is how jazz musicians know what to do next, even though nobody has planned anything or said anything' – but it will be just words. But if you get up close and personal to the dancers and the conductors and the musicians then you may get an 'aha!' moment. You may suddenly just 'get' something, at a gut level. This won't work for all of you in every exercise, but it will work in some exer- cises, and when it does, you will find that something quite simple but quite profound has changed in you, and that 'something', which you might actually find hard to put into words, will really help you to work better with your colleagues and the rest of your organization to get extraordinary results."

Mark stopped talking and looked around the table at the delegates. Roger looked sceptical. Margaret and John looked interested and slightly excited. Rory looked a little bemused. Andrew looked as though he was doing mental arithmetic in a different place, which, sadly, he was.

"Are you ready for your first experience?" asked Mark.

Andrew's eyes came back into focus. "Ah. Yes. What happens now?" he asked, trying to look as if he had been hanging on Mark's every word.

"We are going to talk to an actor about creating ensembles," said Mark.

He led the team out of the room and down several corridors to a larger conference room. Waiting to greet them was Piers Ibbotson, former actor and assistant director with the Royal Shakespeare Company.

Piers has friendly, dark eyes; he is pleasant, thoughtful and listens carefully to what people say. He is modest about his highly successful career and has nothing obviously 'actorly' about him. Piers is quite hard to describe: medium build; medium height; a decent head of dark hair worn short and greying at the temples; good looking without being strikingly handsome.

"Ladies and gentlemen, welcome," said Piers. "My name is Piers Ibbotson. First and foremost, I think of myself as an actor. I acted for many years with the Royal National Theatre and the Royal Shakespeare Company, where I became assistant director in 1990. I have done work in TV and film. But I trained as a scientist and I used to work for the oil industry before I turned to acting."

The delegates stirred a little in their chairs and smiled to themselves with surprise.

"So I know quite a lot about the world of business and about where you are likely to be coming from, and I certainly know a lot about acting and directing, and I have thought long and hard about the connections between the two worlds. And that's what we are going to explore this afternoon and tomorrow.

"Towards the end of my time with the Royal Shakespeare Company," continued Piers, "I got involved with one of our sponsors, Allied Domecq, and I started doing work on management development and consultancy for them, using what I know about theatre and about what performing artists do and what makes them tick, and relating that to management and to business and to leadership. I am still doing that kind of work, with a wide range of blue chip clients, and I contribute to development programmes at several leading business schools, like this one."

"I'd like to start by planting a question in your minds, because it tends to be the first question that occurs to me when I meet a client: 'what is the project you are currently working on, and who is on it?' It sounds like a simple question, and it probably should be, but usually it isn't. 'What are you trying to do?' That's always the question, and it's not always answered satisfactorily."

Piers looked around at the delegates. "What is the project, and who is on it?"

The team exchanged glances.

"I mean, if you're not trying to do anything, if you're humming along, you know – if, to relate this to the world of theatre, the show is up and running and people are coming and paying their money and you're covering your overheads – then you don't necessarily need to do anything. Things are pretty good. I don't know how long you can hum along for before..."

Piers paused.

"Thinking in terms of the theatre again, it's very difficult for a show to stay happy for more than a couple of years, then it needs to be recast and re-rehearsed. Timeframes might be different in business, but nobody can keep on doing the same thing, in the same way, indefinitely. So, if you want to do something different – start a new show, change the current show – then you'd need to plan that as a project. Where are you trying to innovate? What are you trying to make? What do you imagine you want to do differently?

"Now I'm going to take a leap in the dark and assume that because you are all sitting here, there is probably something that you feel you need to do differently."

Piers looked around the group with his rather disconcerting gaze.

"Don't worry! We're not going to talk about it now. But you should talk later with Mark about what the new show needs to look like, if there is to be a new show. What isn't working about the old show? Which bits don't the audience like? Which bits seemed to work well in rehearsal but fall flat on their face when offered to an audience? Because that's one of things that I'm going to argue: a lot of things go into the making of a theatrical performance from a lot of people – the scriptwriter, actors, director, designers, lighting crew, you name it. But there's one other vital partner in all of this: the audience. The audience plays a vital role in the creative process. It is only in the moment of contact between an artwork and the audience that the thing comes to life and acquires meaning and power. So all we luvvies might think the show is absolutely bloody marvelous, darling!" Everyone laughed. "But if it fails to connect with the audience it falls flat on its face and the show dies. And that, I would suggest, applies to all of you, in exactly the way that it does to all performing artists. Work in the modern world has relatively little to do with engineering, and a lot more to do with relation-ships; deals; experiences; visions; pleasures; reassurance."

Piers looked at his audience inquisitively.

"Would you agree?"

Rory was unable to contain himself.

"Well, we like to think that the engineering has something to do with it," he said in his soft, clear Edinburgh accent. "That's what we produce – great engineering."

"Of course you are right, Rory, thank you. But what happens next? Your marvelous products are like a wonderful script; they have great potential – but it's only potential: they are words waiting to be spoken; a show waiting to be brought to life. Any business may have wonderful products, but it's not just the products that the client or the consumer buys: it's the whole show; the whole performance. Products are just the starting point between the makers and the consumers; between the performers and the audience. I might love your product, for example, but hate the system I have to deal with in order to get at the product. That happened to me recently when I went to buy a computer that I am perfectly happy with, but my experience of buying that computer at a retail outlet was a complete nightmare. Does that ring a bell?"

There were nods and smiles amongst the group.

"And then if your lovely new computer goes wrong, you find yourself jumping through all kinds of hoops in an attempt just to get someone to fix it, preferably not at your expense! Yes?"

More nods and smiles.

"So your product might be wonderful, in terms of its engineering and its quality, but my total experience of your product and your company might be more nuanced. So I could say that the play was excellent, but I didn't actually enjoy this performance. And that could be because I didn't like the actors, or the staging, or the interpretation, but it might also be because my seat was uncomfortable and I had a poor view of the stage and there was a big bloody queue for the bar in the interval. So it's the whole *performance* that matters. One bum note or one performance that doesn't gel with the whole ensemble; someone who's just ignoring or riding roughshod over their fellow performers, it ruins everything. Do you agree? It's about the performance of the whole ensemble; it's about everyone who's involved.

"I was once working with a senior manager of a major financial consultancy, and he said to me, 'Do you know, if we could get rid of egos, we'd make millions.' The basis of ensemble work is a level of intense and committed trust. And not the kind of trust that takes years to develop; it's perfectly possible to develop this kind of trust with someone you don't know well or don't even like. What it does need is a kind of emotional strength and a level of humility to lower your emotional defences and allow your fellow members into the ensemble space. You have to experience the very simple trust of giving and receiving. We're not talking about, 'do I trust this person with my life, or my money?' It's more like, 'do we both want this work done well? Can I open myself up to this person so that we can do whatever it takes to see this project carried out marvelously?' And in a real ensemble, everyone is equal before the task: it doesn't matter if you have one line in the play or if you're the main character, you bring the same level of concentration, the same level of passion and commitment. The wonderful thing is – please trust me on this – when you surrender control, when you develop this trust, then you get action; lots of it. When you agree to indulge one another other, nobody is indulgent; the energy that you waste on struggling egos goes straight into the task at hand. Believe me!"

Piers looked around the group.

"When you succeed in building a real ensemble – and it takes effort and time; it involves the kind of things we are about to do here today – you will see a great burst of energy and creativity. But, in my experience, the world of business is uncomfortable with the idea of this. Business likes action. The idea of spending time actually forging a team, building an ensemble, is seen as indulgent. You know – 'well I'm sure that's a lovely idea and we would do it if we had time but we need to get on with things.' Or, 'well, we sent everyone off on conference and we employed these guys who ran some team-building exercises, so I think we've covered that.'

The team looked a bit uncomfortable.

"But, anyway," Piers broke off, "on with the show. This morning, ladies and gentlemen, as you may have gathered, I want to talk about ensembles, status and hierarchies. I want to argue that status and hierarchy are incompatible with genuine ensemble work and must be done away with to create genuine equality before the task. I want to argue that real status between people, as opposed to the artificial status created by social structures and organizations, is actually negotiated in the moment as people interact, which is what happens when there is an accident or a catastrophe: you know, when some passer-by turns out to be the person who can lead in that situation. Status is far more fluid and interchangeable than we like to think and can be readily suspended in certain situations – such as 'putting on a show', for example.

"To explore that, we need to get started on some exercises. I need you to go through some fairly simple experiences so that you can really grasp what it is I'm talking about. Are we ready?" he asks briskly, smiling. "Please clear your chairs to the side of the room."

Piers had shifted into 'director' mode, and the delegates responded instinctively, carrying out his instructions without question. Chairs were lifted and moved, and the large room was cleared for action.

"Now, these exercises are best done with a few more people involved, so I have asked some members of our excellent general staff to join us." Piers went to the door of the conference room and welcomed four members of the business centre's marketing and administrative staff.

"Right, let's get some physical movement going on," said Piers. "Please just walk around the room, trying not to bump into each other."

The group milled around the room, with Piers setting quite a brisk pace, which the group unconsciously took up.

"Change direction from time to time, keep moving. Let's just get a bit loosened up," said Piers, his voice effortlessly filling the room.

"Right, thank you," he said, after about a minute. "Now I have here some of the tools of my trade."

He collected a bundle of bamboo canes, each about four feet long, from the side of the room – the kind of canes that gardeners use to support plants.

"Now we're going to explore moving around while being linked to someone else."

Pier asked the group to form pairs. Without any instruction, the team all chose a 'neutral' partner – one of the business school staff, or Mark Powell - rather than matching up with one of their colleagues. Piers asked the pairs to stand a few feet apart from each other, and to balance one of the bamboo canes on their heads so that it formed a bridge between them. Several canes fell to the floor and there was some embarrassed laughter as they were picked up and re-balanced.

"Now," said Piers, "begin to move around. It doesn't matter which way, just move around and keep the canes on your heads."

The five pairs moved cautiously around the room. Margaret had teamed up with Mark. First Margaret took the lead, moving off to her left, with Mark following. They came to a stop, and Mark moved backwards. Margaret followed. She moved to her right but Mark did not pick up the signal quite quickly enough. The cane fell to the floor. They made good-humoured expressions of annoyance and self-deprecating gestures, picked the cane up, rebalanced it on their heads and started again. In the early stages, Margaret tried to maintain constant eye contact with Mark, which became a little uncomfortable. She found it more effective to keep a general focus on Mark, with occasional eye contact.

"How did we find that?" said Piers, turning to Rory, who had been teamed up with a young woman from the business school's marketing department.

"Well, it was difficult!" said Rory. "It would go well for a bit, then one of us would do something that the other hadn't anticipated, and we would lose it."

"John?"

"We thought we'd got into a rhythm for a bit there," said John, nodding at his male companion from the school's finance department. "And then we lost it. But for a while we were doing pretty well!"

"Right," said Piers. "Now change partners." With the change, some of the team were now partnered with a colleague. Rory found himself teamed up with Andrew, and John was partnered with Roger. Margaret found herself with a young man from the business school's general admin department.

Whereas John's partnership with the unknown man from the business school's finance department had been relatively successful, being partnered with Roger seemed more difficult. The two of them were uncomfortable sustaining any level of eye contact. John found it difficult to follow Roger's movements and involuntarily began to suspect Roger's intentions. Was he deliberately making unexpected moves? John tried to signal his moves clearly, but Roger seemed unwilling to respond or engage. They smiled ruefully at each other as the cane fell from their heads many times. Roger's body language suggested that the thought that the whole exercise was pointless, and beneath his dignity.

Rory and Andrew seemed to be doing better; there was some good natured banter between them when the cane fell to the floor, and they seemed to be enjoying themselves. They held the cane on their heads for a good 40 seconds in one session, moving around the floor quite freely, and then both laughed and threw up their hands in dismay when they finally lost the connection and the cane fell to the floor.

"Ok, stop!" calls Piers. "How was that? Was it different?"

"It didn't work so well this time," volunteered Margaret. 'We didn't seem able to anticipate each other so well."

The woman from marketing who had been paired with Rory said that it seemed easier this time. "Maybe it's just practice," she suggested.

"Practice helps. It's about forging a good connection," said Piers. "Sometimes that comes easily and sometimes it takes a lot of work. But you absolutely can forge that connection, have that bond of complete mutual trust, with someone that you don't know or don't even like. You don't have to like each other, but you have to be there for each other.

"When you act with someone, you need to be present for them, in the moment, and you need to be acutely conscious of what they are doing. You do your bit, you offer something, and they must accept it and take it on. You must be absolutely equal before the task. In any theatrical ensemble, there is likely to be someone who is a more famous actor: you know, someone who is potentially 'grand'. Well, if they run around being 'grand' then it is impossible for that ensemble to work. The best that can happen is that the piece will become a showcase for the grand talent. But truly great actors don't do that. They don't do status in the ensemble. They're conscious of the help and support the ensemble is giving them.

When you watch a really good actor accepting an award, the first thing they will say is 'I couldn't have won this without the support of the wonderful cast.' And when you work with a great actor they give you a great deal too. You raise your game. You do your best work when you are working with someone who is really good. It brings out the best in you.

"Right, let's put the sticks away for now," said Piers, moving around the group and collecting the canes.

"That exercise gave us an idea of what it's like to work with someone at an absolutely basic, physical level. Now let's look at body language with a bit more social context. I'd like you to mingle together as if at a cocktail party, and exchange a few words – you know, 'I'm Piers, I do a bit of acting and a bit of consulting, what do you do? Oh really? That's interesting.'"

Everyone laughed.

"And then after an exchange of pleasantries," continued Piers, "I want you to move on and talk to someone else for a minute or two, and then move on again until I call a halt. OK? Everyone happy with that?"

The group nodded, slightly uneasily.

"When you do this exercise I want you to try to maintain eye contact. You don't have to stare into each other's eyes for three minutes, but try to maintain eye contact most of the time. Ok? Let's go."

The room began to hum with conversation.

"Right, stop!" said Piers after a few minutes. "I want you to carry on with the same kind of conversations but now avoid eye contact. Off we go!"

The same kind of social hubbub ensued, though it was noticeably more subdued. The gathering began to look very uncomfortable. Most people looked down in order to avoid eye contact. Arms were folded.

"OK," said Piers, calling a halt. "What was the difference?"

"I know it's silly", said one of the business school staff, "but I found it impossible to remember the name of the person I was talking to. I also found it harder to concentrate on what they were saying."

"When we *were* looking at each other," said John there was a bit too much eye contact sometimes, and that made me slightly aggressive; I sometimes felt like I was being stared down. But without any eye contact, it felt weird."

"I found it really difficult without eye contact," said Margaret. "I felt the other person was being evasive and I couldn't trust what they were saying. And I agree, it was much harder to stay focused on what they were saying – I kept drifting off!"

"The point is that eye contact really matters," said Piers. "When you are comfortable with somebody there will be a lot of eye contact and you won't even notice. Sometimes people look you in the eye and it feels as if they're making a statement – as John said; it can be challenging. But when there is no eye contact, we find it hard to trust people. All we need to note right now is that it matters. Right, next exercise."

Piers stood in the centre of the room, and all eyes turned to him. He beckoned to Mark Powell.

"Mark, could you come over here?"

Mark moved towards Piers, who suddenly drew himself up, and held his hand up in front of him like a traffic policeman stopping a car.

"Stop!" he barked.

Mark instinctively stopped.

"Right!" said Piers loudly, like a sergeant major. "Come forward!" Mark moved forward a few steps.

"Stop!" barked Piers, then asked, "how are you feeling, Mark?" with a twinkle in his eye.

"Well, I'd very much like to hit you," replied Mark, with a forced smile.

"Status and hierarchy is all around us," Piers explained. "It can play out in many ways, but it's very hard to escape. What Mark and I just did was pretty clear, and, surprising as it may seem, Mark didn't enjoy it very much!"

Everyone laughed.

"Status is normally expressed much more subtly than that. I'm going to give you all a playing card, anything between a three and a king of spades. If you get a king, you are the highest status person in the room. If you get a three, you are the lowest. Let's do the cocktail party routine again, and I want you to display what you feel is the correct body language for your status. If you're a jack or a queen or a king, imagine you are a senior executive talking to a less senior executive. If you are a three or a four imagine that you are pretty much at the bottom of your organization's social ladder. Adjust your body language accordingly." Piers looked down at the floor, let his hands hang down in front of him and shuffled around in a parody of low status. People laughed, a little uneasily.

"At the end, I'm going to ask you to line up according to what you believe your rank to be. So the King and the three know they should be at each extreme, King here and three here," Piers indicated different sides of the room.

"Try to talk to everyone and work out whether they are your superior or inferior in terms of social status."

The group received their cards and started to mingle. Some cast down their eyes and adopted clearly subservient body postures. Some strutted around, talked more loudly than they would normally and adopted forced and superior smiles. Others looked relatively normal. There was a lively interchange for many minutes.

"Thank you" said Piers. "Now take your place in the line according to what you think is the status denoted by your card."

There was a certain amount of last minute checking; some people quickly took positions near to one of the extremes. Several people struck up new conversations before placing themselves in positions in the middle rankings. There was also some uncertainty at the very top of the scale. Margaret, who had in fact been given a card showing the queen, found it hard to decide who exactly held the card showing the king. It was, in fact, the young man from the business school's finance department, who had displayed his utter confidence in his social status by being charming to everyone and declining to strut about in a show of classic male dominance.

The line of people were asked to show their cards. The ranking was nearly perfect.

"It's always amazing how nearly exactly right people get this," said Piers. "It's pretty easy at the bottom, because poor old number three just has to show that they are utterly subservient to everyone else."

Piers did his eyes down, hands down shuffle again. Everyone laughed.

"It can be tough at the top because if you are actually the king, you can behave however you like, right?" Piers smiled at the young man holding the card showing the king. "You may not feel the need to be especially overtly dominant. But the middle is where the real action is. Are you number seven or number eight? It really matters!"

The group smiled wryly.

"The point I want to make," says Piers, "is that we are exquisitely conscious of social hierarchy. And in most modern organizations, status and hierarchy are built into the very fabric of the organization. Everyone knows exactly where they stand in the pecking order.

"But – and this is the point I'm driving at – status and hierarchy are deadly to the ensemble; they are deadly to creativity. When we approach a project – you will find that I'm a bit obsessed with the notion of 'the project', because in the theatre everything is a project – so, in terms of 'the project', status and hierarchy must be stripped out. The team members working on the project have to be equal before the task, otherwise there will be no creativity. And in terms of business, of course, 'creativity' means innovation – which can be a new or changed product, but more often it is just doing things differently: thinking about what the real desired end result is, what you're really trying to achieve, and thinking about different ways of getting there."

Piers looked around at everyone and smiled.

"Now I'd like to explore the idea of creative constraints and the role of the 'director' or leader," he continued. "Leaders of creative ensembles need to be in charge – obviously – but they shouldn't actually be 'in control'. Encouraging autonomy and creativity will give you commitment and enthusiasm, but you lose control of the details. Gaining control of the detail will generally lose you commitment and enthusiasm. So you have a choice: control or creativity?

Detail or enthusiasm? For me, this is the core challenge facing most modern organizations. We are terrified not be to be completely 'in control' because of the pressure not to foul up, but at the same time we desperately need creativity, enthusiasm and commitment. And, in my experience, what we need to generate a high-energy, innovative environment are creative constraints, as opposed to controlling restraints. If you give people a long list of things they can't do, that just stifles enthusiasm. And even if I give you a very loose brief, like 'build something out of these cardboard boxes', that's not very inspiring. You have autonomy, but you don't know where to start or what a good result would look like. But if I give you a creative constraint and say 'use these boxes to make an elephant that dances', then I may have given you a bit of inspiration."

"Can I just interrupt there, Piers?" asked Roger.

"Of course!"

"I like to feel that I am in control of my team. In fact, I insist on it. But they are actually very enthusiastic and highly committed. So I don't see why control and enthusiasm are such complete opposites."

"Well, you are clearly a very successful manager," Piers replied carefully, "You are successfully controlling your team while enabling their enthusiasm. But, if we were talking about the theatre, I – as director – would be thinking, 'well, they're doing what I want, and they're all really enthusiastic, but what would they do if I stopped controlling them? What might they surprise me with, that might be better than what I have told them to do?' What do you think?"

Roger shrugged. "Maybe I'm old-fashioned," he said, "but I hate surprises in business."

"Aha!" smiled Piers. "Well, let's try this exercise because it's good fun and it's quite informative."

Piers outlined the task to the group. "All the chairs stacked on this side of the room need to be moved to the other side, as efficiently as possible. I will be timing the exercise." He selected one of the business school staff and appointed them as leader and nominated Roger as the leader's deputy.

"Everyone must do what you say, Roger," said Piers. "Now consult with the team leader and then put your plan into action. But you have to be quick, because then we are going to try it a different way and see who is faster and the clock starts – now!"

Roger and the 'leader' quickly went into a huddle and talked quietly, turning their backs on the group. Then Roger turned to the group.

"OK. Form a human chain! Two people collecting chairs here. Four people in the chain. The collectors bring the chairs to the chain; you guys pass them hand to hand. Two people at the other end stacking the chairs as they arrive. Everyone got that? Let's go!"

Roger helped direct people into their places; once chairs began to flow from one side to the other, he moved up and down the line, encouraging people. The 'leader' from the business school staff stood to one side, looking on.

"Come on guys, faster!" shouted Roger. Chairs were arriving to be stacked faster than the two stackers could cope with them. As the last chairs arrived with the stackers Roger called for everyone to help stack the remaining chairs.

"We're done!" Roger shouted to Piers as the last chair was stacked. Piers made a show of noting the time involved.

"Very good: 4 minutes, 22 seconds," he announced. "Could you all gather round me? Now we're going to try something else. Forget everything about the last task. It never happened, ok? You are, in fact, at a very posh garden party."

"We haven't got any posh friends," joked John. "We're from Luton!"

"You have a posh friend now!" laughed Piers. "You are drinking champagne and eating canapés in their lovely garden. It's your friend's garden party. You love this person. Also they're your only posh friend, right?"

Everyone laughed.

"We are in a marquee, drinking our champagne, and those chairs are outside, ready for us to have lunch on the lawn. They are very expensive, like everything else in this house. The seats are made of silk damask. But in a minute, there is going to be a sudden thunderstorm!"

Piers looked up dramatically and mimed alarm and horror, holding out his hands to feel imaginary rain.

"Your dear friend calls for your help. 'We have to save the chairs!' Are you ready?"

Everyone nodded. There was some nervous laughter.

Piers moved to the desk at the front of the room that housed the computer. The large double screens had been showing the logos of the business school and the delegates' company. Piers called up the computer's desktop and located a video file. It began to play, showing a wooded parkland not unlike the one outside the conference room, with mature trees and grassy parkland, and a glorious blue sky, dotted with clouds.

"OK, everyone. Start chatting. Drink champagne. Eat canapés."

Everyone started to chat and to drink from imaginary glasses. Conversations were bit stilted at first, but after a couple of minutes people began to relax and talk more naturally.

On the screens, the sky began to darken. There was a distant rumble of thunder, then another: closer; louder. The sky was now filled with dark threatening clouds. The trees began to move in the wind.

A loud clap of thunder and a flash of lightening made everyone jump involuntarily. The sudden hiss and splash of heavy rain filled the room.

Piers ran to the centre of the group, gesticulating wildly.

"It's raining!" he shrieked. "The chairs! They'll be ruined! Please help me everyone!"

With Piers's dramatic prompting the group rose to the occasion and rushed out into the imaginary rain, grabbing chairs at random. Piers rushed around, his hands over his head to ward off the imaginary rain. He winced as thunder crashed again from the sound system. Somehow, Piers managed to look soaked to the skin. He fueled the sense of panic with cries of alarm and exhortation.

"Oh, no! The chairs! Everyone! Please! This is terrible. Oh, thank you, thank you! Yes, in there, out of the rain! Oh, dear! That's right! Thank you so much!"

Nobody suggested any kind of system. Individuals grabbed chairs and ran back 'inside'. Someone meeting someone else halfway as they rush towards them with a chair shouted, "I'll take that! You go back for more!"

Not everyone rose to the drama. Roger managed to remain slightly aloof, as if all of this was rather beneath him. Margaret, John, Andrew and the business school staff did a fine job, rushing around and shrieking, grabbing chairs at random and hauling them back 'inside'. Rory began to catch the mood and joined in, smiling broadly.

When all the chairs had been brought 'inside'. Piers noted the time, stopped the video and called a halt.

"OK. Well, by my stopwatch, the 'thunderstorm' approach was 20 seconds quicker," said Piers, "but then there was no planning time, and the chairs are inside but all over the place, whereas the first team stacked them all quite neatly. But, more importantly, how did you feel about the tasks?"

"Well, the second task was a lot more fun," said Rory, slightly sheepishly. "When we did the human chain, I thought, 'well, that was reasonably efficient'. It was like what we do at the factory every day of our lives. There's always satisfaction when you get it right. But with the rain and the thunder I thought…."

He trailed off.

"You thought?" nudged Piers.

"Well, we were working as a group. So maybe it was chaotic, but we all did our best," said Rory, slightly defiantly, his head up. "I know it's just a game, but there was a crisis and we solved it together. I felt that we were all in it together."

"So," asked Piers, "if you had to think of a way of improving the first task, the human chain task, what would you do?"

After a pause, John spoke up. "Well, I think the human chain was the right solution. But in this size of room, maybe we could have had one less person in the chain, and more people stacking. We'd have to trial that, but we could maybe shave the time a bit."

"And if we had to improve the second, thunderstorm approach?" asks Piers.

Everyone talked at once.

"Maybe we should have formed a chain."

"Maybe we should have just sat on the chairs to keep them dry."

"We could have put some plastic sheeting over the chairs instead of carrying them in."

"But we didn't have any."

"Well, who says!? We could have 'made up' some plastic sheeting! 'Oh, look what I've found! Some plastic sheeting!'" Everyone laughed.

Piers signalled a halt.

"Here's my take on this. When you conduct a task in a managerial, hierarchical sort of way, like in the first exercise, if you want to do it differently, for whatever reason, you have to stop, think and do some planning, then come back with the new idea and try again. But creative leadership thinks as it works. The leadership is shared and anyone can have a good idea. The team will naturally come up with different ways of doing things, and because they're not just following orders, they are involved and they are doing it, they get a deeper understanding of the problem. Do you see?"

Piers looked around at everyone enquiringly. "Ok. Thank you very much everyone," he concluded, wrapping up the session. "We will meet again this afternoon, and I have some other ideas to run past you, but no exercises this time!"

Several people made groans of mock disappointment and smiled. Piers and Mark noticed that Roger said, 'good', not quite under his breath.

"Actually, I lied," said Piers cheerfully. "I do have a couple more exercises for you!" Everyone laughed, except Roger.

"Right, let's get some coffee," said Mark.

Perform to Win

- Modern business is not just about products but also about experiences, visions, pleasures and values – like the performing arts.

- Individual performances receive the support of the whole ensemble; no performer can be brilliant on their own.

- The audience affects the performance and is the final judge of success; performances are judged as a whole and every aspect matters.

- Ensembles need emotional openness and trust to enable creativity; true ensembles suspend hierarchy and status to create equality before the task.

- Successful ensembles need creative constraints from someone who is in charge but not in control.

- When organizations 'plan and implement' they need to stop and rethink when change is needed; creative leadership thinks as it works because everyone is involved.

All That Jazz

Mark led the delegates out of the conference room. "We're going to a different part of the building," he said, as he led the way. "Somewhere we can make some noise and not disturb too many people. I hope!" Mark grinned. "We're going to get some coffee and listen to some jazz. And then, after lunch, we're going to get back together with Piers for the second half of his session."

They walked down a long corridor that opened out into a large open area surrounded by bookcases, with sofas and chairs grouped around occasional tables, and a number of desks with computers on their otherwise empty surfaces. A few people were working at the computers; one group was sitting on sofas engaged in conversation. The team crossed the area and walked down another corridor, emerging into a small conservatory built onto the side of the house. At one end of the conservatory a space had been cleared for a drum kit, an electric keyboard, a double bass, and some brass instruments on stands. A group of musicians sat at a table drinking coffee. As the group arrived, one of the musicians got up to greet them. Mark shook him by the hand and introduced him to the team.

"Ladies and gentlemen, this is Brian. He's put the band together for us today, and he's going to talk to us a bit about jazz and how jazz musicians work together. But mainly he and the guys are going to play some music for us."

The musicians left their table, smiling at the group, and took their places at their instruments. The team helped themselves to coffee and tea from a table at the side of the room and sat down at the nearby tables.

"Good morning everyone," said Brian. "Let me introduce you to the band. This is Colin on keyboards and Martin on drums."

The drummer plays a short drum roll followed by a crash on his hi-hat cymbal.

"Thank you, Martin!" smiled Brian.

"Over here we have Michael on the upright bass." Brian gestured to the bass player, and then turned to the man standing beside him. "And here we have Alan on trumpet. My name is Brian, and I play saxophone – mainly tenor, but also soprano," he said, nodding at the saxophones on a stand beside him.

"We'd like to get things started just by playing you a piece of music, and then I think Mark would like to talk about how we function as a unit – about how jazz musicians work together."

"That's the plan," agreed Mark. "But before you guys start I'd like to point out that you have never played together before this morning, is that right?"

"Yes, that's right," said Brian. "This is just a bunch of guys I was able to get together for this session today. We do all know each other. I've done gigs with Alan and with Colin …" Brian indicated the trumpeter and the keyboard player, "but we're not a regular outfit. We're all professionals, so we make a living doing recording sessions for albums or broadcast, and we may have a regular gig from time to time. All of us do, in fact, play in various jazz line-ups, for fun – it's just not this jazz line-up!" Brian and the band smiled.

"So you've never rehearsed what you're about to play?" asked Mark.

"They don't need to know that!" said Brian in mock horror. "But no. We're going to play some jazz standards that we all know, but that's it."

"In your own time, gentlemen, thank you!" said Mark.

The band started to play John Coltrane's 'Moment's Notice'. The tempo was fast, with a lively, irrepressible beat that lifted everyone's mood. The drum and bass drove the song along, the bassist pluck-ing the strings of his double bass to the beat, his left hand moving rapidly up and down the neck of his instrument as he followed the chord sequence. The song began with a lilting, upbeat melody from the tenor sax; the trumpet joined the saxophone to play a slow, simple phrase in harmony while the bass repeated one high, ring-ing note, suddenly dropping to the same note one octave lower, when, without any apparent signal, the band stopped playing and the piano filled the gap with a tumbling cluster of notes. The band restarted with the main melody, everyone playing the heavily syn-copated tune together. The saxophone played a soaring phrase that was one of the most memorable features of the song – the team would find themselves humming this to themselves on occasions for the rest of the programme – and then the bass repeated the one high note and the song came to one of its sudden brief halts before moving into a series of solos from the members of the band. As the players improvised in turn around the chord sequence of the song, other members of the band occasionally picked up and reflected some particular turn of phrasing or rhythmic pattern from the soloist. The whole band seemed to be focused on pushing each soloist along; supporting and encouraging him. At what seemed to be entirely unpredictable moments, the band came to one of the sudden, dramatic brief stops, before the music was picked up again by the next soloist. At the end of the piano solo, without any intervening gap and without any signal, the whole band launched back into the core melody, the saxophone played its soaring phrase for a final time and the song came to an end.

The team gave a warm round of applause.

"Thank you," said Brian.

Mark turned to the team. "I don't know if any of you are jazz fans at all?" he asked.

"I had a spell of listening to a lot of jazz when I was a student," said John, "so I'm a kind of fan, but I'm certainly not an expert!"

"I love Ella Fitzgerald," said Margaret. "Does that count?"

"It surely does!" smiled Brian.

"So what were you playing there?" Mark asked Brian.

"Well, that was a piece written by John Coltrane," replied Brian. "And that's pretty firmly in the bebop camp. What we tend to think of as jazz started with musicians taking a known tune and then improvising around it. And in the early days, the solos were very melodic. They were literally a kind of improvisation on a theme, and then what became known as bebop introduced faster tempos, the improvising became much freer and more edgy, and the melody was often just a short theme to form the basis of the improvised piece. So the main point of the piece, really, was to give individual players a chord sequence to improvise over – the melody was just a starting point. So when we talk about jazz…" (Brian gestured at the other players around him), "that's what we tend to mean. A small ensemble improvising over a known sequence."

"Can I ask what struck anybody most about watching the guys play?" Mark asked the team.

There was a slight delay, then John spoke up.

"Guys, can I just say how much I enjoyed that? I'm a bit of a jazz fan, as I was saying, though I don't listen to much of anything these days." He paused. "But I'm not a musician and I've never really understood how jazz works. It's great seeing you guys so close up.

"The first thing I wanted to say was that you were all clearly having such a good time! You were enjoying every second of it – I could see all of you taking a great deal of pleasure in each other's performance. Really! And I'm afraid if you watched us working together, it wouldn't look as if we were having that much fun – which is a terrible shame."

"Sometimes we have fun!" said Margaret.

"Yes, that's sort of what I mean, Margaret," agreed John. "Business can be fun, but maybe we don't feel that we should look as if we're having fun!"

"Well, playing jazz is fun," said Brian. "We play jazz because we love it, and we tend to make most of our money playing other stuff. So when we play together the whole point is to do your absolute best, and to help the other guy to do their absolute best; you know, to inspire them in some way. So when Alan is soloing on his trumpet I am, first of all, jealous!" The band all laughed. "Because he's so good. And then I'm inspired! It's great. It fires off ideas in my head and I think 'oh, yes, I could do something with that; that's brilliant!' And it's the same with the rest of the band. On that last piece, Martin and Michael …" – Brian indicated the drummer and bass player – "were really pushing us along. Giving us a lovely platform but also suggesting some interesting rhythmic possibilities. And that's like heaven. That's what it's all about. So, if we're smiling, it's because we really are having a good time! It's about being enabled to play, not just at your best, but doing stuff you wouldn't have thought of on your own. And trying to do the same for the other guys in return and being blown away by what they do."

"Well it's lovely to watch, I can assure you!" continued John. "Can I also ask: in that song there are lots of breaks, and you all stop together, but I have no idea how you do that. How do you know when the break comes?"

"That's not magic," said Brian. "The song – the chord sequence – is a set length. Any tune lasts for a certain length of time, obviously, and in jazz we use the chord sequence that underpins the tune and we play around that. The sequence on this song happens to be 32 bars long and the last two bars are silent. So it's not that hard."

"So, do you count the bars to know where you are?"

"Not really. If you're soloing, then you have to know exactly where you are in the sequence so that you play the right notes. Even though we're creating the music as we go along, we need to know what chord we're playing over. So because you know where you are in the sequence, you know when you get to the end, and you know there's a break. All of the musicians stop for two bars, and the solo-ist fills the space with a little something."

"What about the drummer, can I ask?" said John. "Does he count the bars?"

"Sometimes we do have to count," replied Martin, the drum-mer. "But we tend to 'feel' it. You know, seriously, if you were relying on counting out 30 bars you'd almost certainly lose it." He mimed playing drums, hitting at imaginary drums and cymbals, and counting aloud: "21…22…23…24…25…um." He stopped playing his imaginary drums suddenly and looked around him, startled, as if he had lost his place. Everyone laughed.

"So we 'feel' it," continued Martin. "And you tend to think – or feel – in 4 bar sections, you know; or 8 bars; 16 bars. You just know when you've got to the 16th bar. In long solos though, where there isn't a defined end, you need signals. The next bit might be a reprise of the chorus, and that might need a signal. Sometimes, the soloist does something obvious, like stepping back from the

mic. Often, it's just eye contact or sometimes there's a musical signal. And it can be something like this..." He played a 2 bar drum
break that is clearly leading to a new starting point, and paused
dramatically with his stick in the air at the point when the next
section would begin.

"So some of it is prearranged, and some of it is signalled?"
asked Andrew.

"That's right," agreed Brian. "Jazz is improvisatory, so you have
to have some ground rules that let you play together. That's why we
can play without rehearsal, so long as we know what to expect. In
jazz, you normally play the tune together to kick off, and then you
use the chord sequence as the basis of the improvisation for the rest
of the song. And the tune might be 30 seconds and the improvisation might be 30 minutes, but you know what the foundation is: the
foundation is the chord sequence. The real joy of jazz is that, once
you understand the ground rules, then musicians can get together
and play very good jazz almost off the cuff, and it will be completely unique because they are inventing it moment to moment,
and that is possible because they understand the framework."

"When you are improvising, how do you know what to play
to sound good?" asked Rory. "I mean, I can just about imagine
making up a new tune and playing it, but what if it doesn't fit
the music?"

"Ah, tough question!" said Brian, smiling. "Alan?"

"That's the million-dollar question," Alan admitted. "The one
thing you *don't* want to play is anything you've played before. We
all have certain stock phrases that we know will work in certain
situations. And there's a terrible temptation to wheel those out
when you're not feeling inspired. Even the best players do it: you
know, you're listening to a great solo but then you think 'I've heard
that before!'"

The band laughed.

"I guess one answer," Brian contributed, "is that we know the
chord sequence of the song, and we know from practise and the-
ory what notes you can and can't play against a chord. And the joy

of jazz is that you can play some notes that really shouldn't work with a certain chord, but they kind of do. Charlie Parker, probably the greatest bebop saxophonist, played at ridiculous tempos over complex chord sequences, and never put a foot wrong. Some old jazzer once said, 'Charlie Parker never played a wrong note in his life'. And it's true! The genius of Parker was that he found an unusual way of putting phrases together that worked against almost any sequence."

"Do you think about the chords and what will fit with them while you are playing?" asked Margaret.

"There isn't time!" said Alan. "If you were trying to think, 'oh, this chord is so-and-so, what's going to work with that?' you'd be in trouble. So when we practise, we do a lot of scales. When I visualize a particular chord in the sequence, my fingers have a memory of that scale and what works and doesn't work. But when you get to be really good ..." "Like Alan!" interrupted Brian. "When you get to be really good," laughed Alan, "you really do 'play it by ear'. You hear the sounds the other players are making and your body just knows what will work musically. You just try to think of a new line that will fit around the sounds you're hearing; you try to create a whole new cool tune on the foundations of the old tune. You want to master your instrument and master the musical structure to the point that anyone can throw pretty much anything at you, and you will be able to respond with something pretty good."

"Does that idea resonate with anyone?" Mark asked the team. "The idea of having mastered your craft to the point where you can do things almost instinctively?"

"Well," offered Rory, "in engineering we're obsessed with testing everything. So we don't really do anything 'live' in quite the same way. But you do get people who are really on top of their game and when you give them a problem, sometimes they can see the answer before they can explain to you – or sometimes even to themselves! – why they know it's going to work."

"I suppose it's a bit like being a master of your brief," ventured Andrew. "You know, when you've got all the facts and figures in your head and it doesn't matter what anybody fires at you, you have the answer. Is that the same thing?"

"Absolutely the same" confirmed Brian. "As a musician, you want to not have to think about any of the technical issues, so that you can focus on the performance."

"Can I ask," said Andrew, "who is leading the band? You were saying that all of you knew when to stop in that last piece, but, who is *directing* the band? Who's the leader?"

"There is no leader," replied Brian. "There might be one guy who pulls the band together, and chooses the repertoire and does most of the organizational stuff, and in terms of putting this group together, that was me. But there's not always even a leader in that sense; sometimes it's very much a cooperative. And, when we actually play, there is no leader. The leadership passes around. When anyone takes a solo, they can take the song in quite different directions. In fact, that's the whole point. They can take it right down and make it much more mellow, or they can jazz it up and really push it along. And it's up to the other players to follow that, and support it. The rhythm section – drums, bass, piano or guitar – need to be very sensitive to what's going on. They can also start things off themselves, you know; they might pick up something that the soloist has done and reinforce it or go off in a new direction that gives the soloists new ideas and more inspiration. That's why you can't really 'rehearse' solos. You know, you can play by yourself in your back room for as long as you like, and its good practice, but it can't be 'a solo' until you're playing with other people. It's the other musicians that make what you do possible. So, to answer the question, in our kind of band, there might be a 'band leader' who is 'in charge', but he's absolutely not 'in control' when we play – the performance depends completely on surprises; it depends on any one of the players doing something new and unexpected and forcing the others to rethink and adapt. If there weren't those constant surprises and challenges, we'd soon end up playing the same thing every night, which is not jazz. Well…" he corrected himself, "it's not our kind of jazz. Big bands, swing bands, absolutely do have a band leader and he or she is up there on the podium conducting the band like an orchestral conductor, but it's also much more of an orchestral performance."

"Colin here, for example, recently gave up a well-paid gig because he got bored!" Brian glanced over at Colin the keyboard player, inviting him to tell his story.

"Well, yes," says Colin. "I got a gig with …" – he named a famous musical – "and it was fun for the first week or so. First of all, you just play the dots; and then you work on your bit to try to make it better. There's maybe a few places where you can add a bit of something without showing off or treading on anyone's toes. And then … that's it. You just keep doing that, night after night. It pays the rent, but it doesn't make me happy. It's not why I play music. So I play with various scratch jazz outfits whenever I get the chance, because that *does* make me happy. You can get a lot of satisfaction out of doing something really well – you know, like the orchestral guys. But it's really hard to keep that feeling night after night in a show. It becomes like a production line, whereas jazz is like an anti-production line. It's like pure freedom. It's energizing."

"Guys," said Mark, "before you play another number can I just ask you to do a little experiment? I'd just like you to play the first piece again, but badly!"

"I guess we can do that," said Brian, smiling.

The band played the same song. Everyone played their part, accurately, but it was immediately obvious to the team that the piece was falling flat. Some sparkle had gone from it. When the set melody ended and the saxophone took the first solo, it wasn't the same. The drummer kept time; the keyboard played the right chords and the bass player kept to the bass line, but the saxophonist was left high and dry; it sounded like an exercise; as if he was playing over a backing tape. The trumpet player took over, but half way through his solo, the band came to a stop, as if by agreement.

"Can we stop doing that now, Mark?" asked Alan, the trumpeter. "That's not fun!"

"Thanks very much guys," said Mark. "I've never heard you play so badly!"

"Thank you, Mark!" said Brian.

"So, were you playing the same things?" asked Margaret.

"Oh yes, same notes and breaks and everything," said Brian. "No real mistakes, as such, just what I think we would call 'cloth ears!'"

The band all laughed.

"So what's happening there," said Mark, "is that the guys have stopped listening to one another; they've become selfish. They've let their egos off the leash. Whereas, when they play normally, their ego is carefully under control; they use it to try to be brilliant, but not at everyone else's expense; in fact, it's the reverse: they try to be brilliant and to help the other guys be brilliant too. But once they stop listening to one other, it's every man for himself, and it goes horribly wrong."

"What was surprising," said Andrew, "was that it was obvious immediately."

"It's that 'ensemble' thing that has gone missing," agreed Mark. "When the ensemble is really working together, everyone is focused on what their fellow players are doing and on helping each other to create a great performance. Once they stop doing that, it's just a bunch of people playing at the same time; it might be technically correct, but it's not a good performance. What's interesting is that, in music, you can hear that straight away. It's obvious. But in business, it's not so easy. That's why I talk about the 'pulse' of businesses. Because although all the metrics might be fine, it's only when you dig deeper that you realize the business isn't functioning properly at all. Yes?"

The team looked thoughtful.

"Ok. Let's let the guys get back to what they were going to do!" Mark smiled at the band. "Brian, what have you got for us next?"

"We have a little demonstration about improvisation. We're going to improvise something from scratch. So this isn't an existing song. We're going to play whatever comes into our heads, and then try to work together with that. I hope it'll sound ok, and demonstrate that we can even take away the foundation of a known chord sequence and still make good music."

The rhythm section established a tempo and, after some exploratory chords and phrases from the piano, seemed to settle on a key. The saxophone and trumpet player played various phrases, sometimes playing at the same time. The piece had a lot of energy but sounded a bit disjointed; the various elements didn't quite seem to come together into a satisfying whole.

Then there was a perceptible shift. The bassist seemed to settle into a pattern with the keyboard player. The drums began to push the rhythm forward confidently. The saxophone launched into a flowing improvisation with a satisfying shape and feel. The trumpet seamlessly took over the lead and reached a natural close at which the keyboard also stopped, leaving the bass player to solo while the drums subsided to a minimal pattern, keeping the beat and picking up the odd accent. At some signal that the team all missed, the band came back in with what now sounded like a familiar theme; the trumpet weaving a kind of counterpoint around the saxophone. The piece came to an end, the sax breaking into a cascade of notes over the final chords and the drummer bringing everything to a final close with a series of flourishes.

The team applauded enthusiastically.

"Wow. Thanks guys," said Mark. "Any thoughts anyone?"

"So that was off the top of your heads?" asked Margaret. "It wasn't based on anything else?"

"No, that was just improvised," confirmed Brian.

"And it seemed to kind of pick up," said John. "There was a point where it seemed to come together more."

"You're very kind!" laughed Alan. "Yes, we did get into a bit of a groove after a bit. When everyone's improvising, it can be quite cool, but you're all still feeling your way, and it doesn't really settle. It's all kind of up in the air. Then we might get into a groove, which I guess means something identifiable, something repetitive, even if it repeats over a long period."

"This is probably a silly question," said Rory, "but what's happening in the early stages before you get into the groove?"

"That's actually a very perceptive question, Rory," said Mark. "Brian, do you want to have a go at answering before I add my thoughts?"

"Sure," said Brian. "It is a good question. This is improvisation, so you don't know what's going to happen, and whatever happens, you don't know whether it's going to work or not. We're literally swapping leadership around, letting one person or another explore a particular avenue. We listen carefully to what the other guys are doing and decide what our contribution should be. And that might be to play along with what they have just created – to take the foundation they've offered and embellish it – or do something different that takes it off in a new direction. So it takes a while to get into a groove. The early stuff is exploratory. Hopefully it's quite an enjoyable exploration for the listener, but it hasn't quite achieved a consensus. And I don't mean a show of hands, obviously, but as John said, 'it seemed to come together' – well, that was you hearing the players instinctively pick up on the new direction. You know it's working when you can hear it working and suddenly it works for all of us; it just clicks."

"What I was thinking was also about leadership," added Mark. "You know, you guys...' – he gestured at the band – "are very confident about stepping in and taking leadership. You listen to each other so carefully, and respect what each person does. You're actually quite brave in stepping in and making a new suggestion; in filling the space that someone else has offered with something that takes it further, or somewhere new. In business, in my experience, as soon as someone leaves a space, some idiot will jump in with a pre-prepared bit, regardless of whether it's appropriate or not."

The team smiled in acknowledgement.

"Whereas you guys see that a space is being offered and you know you are entitled to fill that space. That it's allowed, and that it's a contribution; it's a suggestion, not a diktat."

"That's nicely put," said Brian. "We've got one last short piece to play you, and then we'll say goodbye. We're going to play a Charlie Parker song called 'Donna Lee' and it's pretty fast and furious."

The band launched into a fast and complex melody, with the sax and trumpet playing in unison at breakneck speed. It sounded as if they were improvising at high speed in tandem, but it became clear that the long melody was actually scripted. At the end of the melody, the saxophone began to improvise, but instead of playing an extended solo, allowed the trumpet to come in after a few bars. The two traded phrases off each other, sometimes echoing what the other had just done, sometimes going in a new direction. After a minute or so, they slipped seamlessly back into the long, twisting melody line, playing in perfect unison, until the whole band stopped at exactly the same, apparently unpredictable, moment.

There was a round of applause. "Thank you very much!" said Brian.

"Ladies and gentlemen, a big thank you to Brian and the boys," said Mark. "Brian; Colin; Michael; Martin; Alan. Thanks guys."

The team applauded some more to show their appreciation.

"And now," said Mark, leading the team out of the conservatory, "it's time for more drama!"

Perform to Win

- Ensemble players spark off one another's performance: each player's brilliance inspires the others and supplies a stream of new ideas.

- Individual egos are controlled and subsumed to the overall performance; the energy is used to drive the ensemble.

- Mastery creates embodied knowledge; true masters of their craft 'feel' what to do next without analysis.

- True ensembles are leaderless; leadership is shared, allowed and passed around.

- Great ensemble performance is made possible by each individual's intense focus on their fellows, raising performances above 'technically proficient' and introducing real artistry.

- Ensemble players create spaces and invite others to fill them with new ideas.

Too Many Hamlets

Lunch was served in a larger conservatory built against the south face of the great house. Outside the tall conservatory windows, the lawn sloped down to the river.

The group helped themselves to dishes laid out on the serving counter and took their seats at an empty table. Andrew still looked distracted though, in general , the morning's activities had been too engrossing to allow anyone's mind to dwell much on work. John engaged Andrew in a conversation about rubgy, a passion they shared. Margaret talked to Rory about a new technical development at the factory. Roger looked tense and unhappy. He managed to strike up a conversation with a delegate from a different programme who was sitting next to him; the conversation turned quickly to golf.

After lunch, Margaret, Rory, Andrew and John went outside to stretch their legs. Roger left them to use one of the computers in the communal area.

When they were near the river, Margaret turned to John. "What do you think, John? Will it be valuable? The programme, I mean. These three days. Will it be a good use of our time or do you think we should have cancelled the whole thing and stayed back to focus on the re-pitch?"

Andrew and Rory heard Simon's question and stopped their own conversation, waiting for John's reply.

"It's hard not to wish we were back at the office *doing* something," replied John after a pause. "But we all agreed this might throw up something useful. We've got several weeks after we get back to concentrate on the re-pitch. So I'm thinking that we should just submerse ourselves in this, try to stop worrying about what's happening back at the plant and see what we come out with at the end of the three days. I can't say that anything we've done so far has made me think, 'that's the answer!' but that's unrealistic. A few ideas have been interesting. A bit off the wall, but thought-provoking. I'm happy to go with it. What do you think?"

John noticed Rory and Andrew listening intently to their conversation and looked across to include them in the question.

"We're here now," agreed Rory. "And we need all the help we can get. We need new ideas. I'm a bit sceptical, but we might as well see the thing through properly. Andrew?"

"I'm finding it hard to concentrate," said Andrew. "But my team doesn't need me there to crunch numbers. I should relax. I liked the jazz. I don't know what I can do with it, but it was interesting. It's different. And Piers is a clever guy with some interesting ideas. I'm up for it."

"And what about you, Margaret?" asked John.

"Well, the whole programme was my idea, so I feel a bit guilty that we're all here at a time when maybe we wish we weren't. But I really believe it will be valuable for us and help us see things differently. I just wish we weren't in crisis mode at the same time!"

"Let's try to pretend that we're not in crisis mode," said John. "Let's head back and see what they've got for us this afternoon!"

* * *

"Good afternoon!" smiled Piers, once everyone had settled back into the room.

"The exercises we did this morning were mainly about forming ensembles; about recognizing that to create a genuine ensemble where people can trust each other and volunteer new ideas without fear of ridicule or embarrassment, we have to suspend status. We have to be equal before the task.

"This afternoon, there are a number of other key concepts that I would like to talk about – things about the performing arts that I believe are potentially highly relevant to business. Things that performing artists do differently, that people like yourselves may be able to use to your advantage. I have worked with a large number of companies over the years, and I have never known anyone not take something out of these ideas and find it useful.

"So, I'm going to talk for a bit while your lunches go down, before I ask you to do some more exercises. The first thing I would like to talk about is the theatre," Piers continued, "but in a general sense."

Piers brought an image of an operating theatre onto the double screens in the conference room.

"There are a few things that we call theatres," he continued. "The theatre itself, obviously, with the stage as the focal point. But also hospital theatres; war theatres; theatres of action. And all of these theatres have a kind of concentric structure. At the heart of the organization is the theatre where the defining activity of the organization goes on, and the people who are in that theatre are the most important people. They almost certainly aren't the most *senior* people – there will be a few senior people, you know, a great actor, an eminent surgeon, a senior military commander, but these kinds of organization tend to have layers of people built up around them, like the layers of an onion. In general, as you move further away from the centre of the action, those layers get more senior, in terms of status and salary, but the real action is in the theatre. So on the theatrical stage you have the actors, playing their various roles, large and small, but all vital to the action. And then you have a bunch of people who do not actually appear on stage, but who are very close to the scene of action – the dressers, stage managers, scenery guys, lighting technicians and all of that. And they have great kudos because they are so close to that core activity, that symbolic heart of the organization. And they are typically very passionate and committed. As you move away from the centre of action, so people tend to become less passionate, less committed and are certainly seen as being less important, in some fundamental sense. So the chief financial officer of the Royal Shakespeare Company is a very important person, and is paid accordingly, and no doubt they take great pride and pleasure in working for the RSC. But no one would make the mistake of thinking that the CFO was one of the most important people in the RSC.

"We forget at our peril what the beating heart of our organization is and that the people down there are actually what it's about, and even though you may be paid a great deal of money and have a significant role in the company, you really are not that important compared to the people who serve the burgers, for example. They really matter.

"I mean, forgive me, ladies and gentlemen. You all do vital work for your company. But that may not be the same as being on the stage, or being part of the team that makes what happens on the stage happen.

"So there's my first bit of food for thought for you today." Piers looked around the group again. "Where is your theatre of operation? What is the beating heart of your organization? Where is the stage; the battlefield; the operating theatre?"

Rory looked around at his colleagues for support and said, "Well, it's our factories, isn't it? I mean, they're the beating heart of our business. We're an engineering firm; we make things. So the factory is our beating heart."

"Well, it might be," said Piers, thoughtfully. "I mean, I love the idea of exploring your factories as theatres. You know, what is the show we're putting on? What's it called? Who are the main actors? Who are the bit actors? Who is the director? All of that would be fascinating to explore. But 'theatres' are usually where you meet the public. You know, in acting, it's where you show your stuff to the audience. In the operating theatre it's where you deal with the patient; in a theatre of war, it's where you meet the enemy. Someone else is involved and that someone is the whole point of the organization. So I would say that your factories are, obviously, a crucial part of the show but I don't think that they are your 'theatre of operations'. That would need somebody else: a client I guess."

"Well, that's my role," said Roger. "I'm in charge of client relations."

"Absolutely," agreed Piers. "But in that show, you know, you are the lead, you are Hamlet, and your sales colleagues all have leading parts." Piers smiled. "And you get to play to your audiences, to your clients. But that doesn't quite feel like the whole show to me. What about the bit players? If you are Hamlet, where are the servants and the soldiers and the gravediggers? Where are the equivalent of the surgical assistant and the nurse anaesthetist? Where are the tank drivers and the squaddies?

"But that's another question and something you'll want to take up yourselves and perhaps with Mark, later. At the moment I'm just trying to throw out a few ideas, mindsets really, from the world of theatre to see if they're of any use to you guys. At the moment, it's looking hopeful!" He smiled broadly.

"Next thought." Piers moved to the computer and selected the next image. A picture of the promotional poster for Laurence Olivier's 1948 film version of *Hamlet* appeared on the screen. In the poster, Olivier is heavily made up; his hair is cut short and dyed blond, and he is cradling the skull of Yorrick against his cheek.

"Well, we were talking about Hamlet," said Piers. "Here's the chap. Here we have Sir Laurence Olivier, and we all know what play Olivier is in. He's in *Hamlet*. And in fact, he is Hamlet. He's not the gravedigger.

"Now the question of what play we are in and what role we are playing is well worth thinking about. This is a simple point, and I won't labour it," continued Piers, "but for me it is quite profound.

"There's a lot of talk about 'authenticity' and about 'being ourselves', especially in terms of leadership. And there is a very good point at the centre of that, which is that people see through phoniness in a split second. When people are pulling the wool over our eyes, usually they might as well have 'I am lying' written on their forehead. Their body language tells us all we need to know. You know how this works: you see a politician on the TV and what do you think?"

Piers looked at the group.

"You think, 'Is this person telling me the truth?' – right? 'Can I trust them, or are they lying?' And nine times out of ten we think, 'Ah; shifty. Can't trust them.' And that's the end of their reputation with us. All done in a split second. And then you get the exception, the tenth politician who says, 'actually, I don't have a ready answer for that problem. All I can tell you is that I'm going to try my hardest to get it sorted.' Suddenly, we believe them. We may not agree with them, but we think they have principles, we think we can trust them. Same, obviously with leadership in business.

"But my point is that we get confused about 'authenticity'; we get confused about our 'real selves'. Actors don't tend to see things in such black and white terms, because we spend a lot of our time being someone else. What I am suggesting is that we are actually many slightly different people. We are not quite the same person at work as we are at home. We are not the same as 'spouse' as we are as 'parent' or as 'friend'. We are not quite the same as 'board member' as we are as 'boss of this division'. Yes?"

The group looked attentive and focused.

"Now, for example, I am currently playing a starring role in the play called *My Family Life*. And the starring role is 'dad' – the most important role in the show, obviously," said Piers, smiling.

"Ha!" snorted Margaret, good-naturedly.

Piers shrugged. "Well…" He laughed. "But, as well as having the starring role as 'dad', I also have a much smaller role as 'father at the school gates', in a play called *My Life At School*, which stars my daughter. And I have to think very carefully about how I play the role of 'father at the school gates', because it's only a walk-on role but it has a devastating effect on the play and on my daughter's performance if I get it wrong – you know, if I make the mistake of thinking that I am the most important person in that show."

"So my second little piece of food for thought is this: 'What play are you in, and what role are you playing?' And the play will change, and your role will change, and I would suggest that you need to adjust your performance quite considerably in each circumstance. Because if you just keep on 'being you' – as in 'oh, I can't help it, that's just the way I am,' then you will make life very difficult for the other performers and can actually do a lot of damage to the show."

Piers changed the image on the screen to an aerial view of a battlefield with tanks, gun emplacements and troops in combat gear.

"Third idea," said Piers. "There are only five ideas I want to run past you, so we're doing well. This is not actually a picture of a battle, it's a picture of a battlefield exercise; a war game. And what I want to talk about is the concept of rehearsal.

"There's a common confusion about rehearsal being a process of practising, which it's not. Rehearsal, in a theatre, is a process of finding out how you're going to do what's written down in the script. You've got a lot of material there already, you've already got the story, you know where you're going, you know what's happening or what you want to happen, you've got the sets, the costumes. You've got all the actors and their personalities and you've also got all of their separate perspectives on their roles. So you've got loads of potential in the room. And a good rehearsal is a managed process for getting everybody to explore all the possible ways in which they could interpret the stuff they have to do, under the supervision of the director. The director is critical. Because the director sits outside that process and observes and nudges and directs, coaches the discussions, the conversations, the attempts. And through that process they select the best solutions to the problems of the scene.

"So you go in with a lot of ideas about what you think it should be like or how it should end up, but you don't know the final outcome. As directors, you've probably got what I call a 'misty vision'. You know, I want it to end up roughly over there, but I don't know how I'm going to get there or exactly what it's going to look like – because of all this is stuff that you…" – Piers looked at the group as if they were the actors in an ensemble that he was directing – "are going to give me. So you set up a safe space where you can say, 'well, what if we do this? Let's try it this way'. And then everybody explores the possibilities of what the implications might be while you watch as the director. And from that material you think, 'ok, it looks like that would be a problem', or 'that's not going to work', or 'this bit works better – so let's try it this way.' And you do it again, scene by scene, section by section through the play, building up the final performance. It's a creative process of discovery. It's not the same as practicing. And this is where the work we did earlier on status is so important, because in *rehearsal*, status has to be left outside the room. You can't offer things; you can't open yourself up emotionally; you can't establish that essential *trust*, if anybody in the ensemble is playing status games. I'm guessing you all know that from experience?"

Piers looked around the group for agreement.

"You've probably experienced meetings where it isn't really a meeting – well, it certainly isn't a rehearsal, a creative process – because someone in the room knows damn well what outcome they want and they make it plain that they outrank you and that there is only one correct answer."

The team shifted a little uncomfortably in their chairs.

"Can I just interrupt for a moment?" asked Mark. "Does that ring a bell with anyone?" He turned to the delegates. "I mean the question of whether businesses ever rehearse properly. In my experience, people practice, but they don't normally rehearse. There are some exceptions. Some very sales-based operations genuinely rehearse: they genuinely role play what they would like to say and how a real client is likely to respond. The implementation of some IT systems is rehearsed, to try to spot likely issues. But, in general, we practice, but we don't rehearse. Not creatively. "

"I think that's a fair point," agreed John after a pause. "We run through stuff all of the time, but I guess it's more like learning our lines."

"Well, there is an element of rehearsal in design," said Rory thoughtfully. "You know, when we're designing something, if something doesn't work in practice, then we go back to the drawing board and change it."

"That's a very good example," said Piers. "The design process is a kind of rehearsal. Real rehearsal is about co-creation, it's about incremental development by exploration and the development of ideas. But I gather that, in some businesses, there is this thing called 'the duty to dissent'. You know, when anybody puts up an idea, your duty is to try to shoot it full of holes to prove it's no good. So you get this immensely competitive arena where only the person who's been able to build a cast-iron case and fend off all possible objections is going to win, but their idea might be completely wrong. And since no one else has had any part in framing that idea, nobody apart from that one person or team feels any sense of ownership in that idea. I would like to suggest that every idea is, initially, 'half baked' and that the job of the team, the function of rehearsal, is to try to fully bake the idea, to play around with it and work on it and see if it works. And if it doesn't; then we need another half-baked idea. Do you see?"

"That's clever," said John. "We *are* quite adversarial about ideas. I mean, if you manage to persuade people that your idea is good enough to be listened to, which I'm afraid can be a struggle in itself – I'm not talking about between us here…" – he gestured at his colleagues – "I mean that I'm afraid it can be hard for someone with a bright idea to get it up to a higher level. And then they get to 'present' it with numbers and slides and all the rest of it. And you're right. We tend to pick holes in it. 'That's never going to work', or 'you haven't thought of this', and so on."

"Yes, thank you, John," said Piers. "Can we just try a little exercise to illustrate that? Rehearsal is not the same as improvisation, but it shares some of the same rules. In rehearsal, when an actor offers you something – a tone of voice; a gesture; a facial expression – you need to be open to that. You need to accept it and add something to it through your response; to move it along further and see where it goes. In improvisation – as in any act of co-creation – you have to take away any sense of anxiety about how things will be received. So, in your case, John, I'm guessing those poor people presenting to you would be in a state of considerable anxiety?"

"I'm afraid so," agreed John.

"Yes, indeed," smiled Piers. "And being anxious is very bad for creativity. So, in improvisation and in proper rehearsal, that anxiety is removed because the rules of the game are that every offer is accepted and then embellished: you add your little something to it and then offer it back for further embellishment. The rules of the game are that your reply is 'yes, and…' You accept the offer without embarrassment and you add something. So, for example, if I say to one of you…"

Piers looked around the group and turned to Roger.

"Roger," said Piers, "that's a very smart hat you're wearing!"

Roger looked bemused and slightly irritated. "I'm not wearing a hat," he replied, flatly.

"Now, that was unfair of me," said Piers, "because I haven't really set you up for it. But that's what we call 'blocking.' I have made you an offer in my little improvisation, but you have refused it. It's dead. We can't go any further with it. Now let's have another go."

Piers turned to Margaret.

"Margaret, that's a lovely hat you're wearing!"

"Oh, do you like it?" Margaret replied brightly. "I have to go to a wedding later."

Piers smiled broadly.

"Now we're in business!" he said. "To a wedding? A friend of yours?"

"Well, definitely a friend but not quite a wedding, in all honesty," replied Margaret, turning to John sitting beside her. "John and his wife Elizabeth are renewing their vows. It's very sweet." She smiled mischievously at John.

"Um, are we?" spluttered John.

"Well, not quite blocking, John, but not quite good enough either!" laughed Piers. "Yes, and…" remember!"

"Um, yes," said John. "Yes, that's right. We are renewing our vows."

"And…?" prompted Piers.

"And it happened to coincide with this three-day workshop, but we thought we'd go ahead anyway."

"And?" Piers raised an eyebrow.

"So that's why I'm wearing a morning suit!"

"Excellent!" said Piers. "And where's your top hat, John?"

"Well, I thought it would be safer to keep it in its box," said John. "What made you decide to wear your hat to these sessions, Margaret?" he asked.

"Well the air conditioning is turned up so high, it's freezing!" replied Margaret. "I'm sure that's why Andrew is wearing his balaclava."

"Excellent!" cried Piers. "Marvelous. I'll stop you there to get poor Andrew off the hook. But you take my point? That was just a bit of improvisation – the only thing we're trying to do there is to try to keep an idea going and have fun. When we are rehearsing, when we are trying to co-create something new and different, we accept everything that is offered, and we try to work with it. And if it doesn't work after we've given it a good run, then we try something else. That's what rehearsal is all about. If you would like to explore this further, I highly recommend a book by Keith Johnstone, called *Impro*.[1] Now here's another thing," said Piers, changing the slide of the battlefield exercise to a photograph of an actor, dressed as a peasant, standing in a freshly dug grave and lifting up a human skull on his spade.

"Now we're back with *Hamlet*, and here we have the first gravedigger, one of two gravediggers, also referred to in the text as 'clowns'. And after the two gravediggers have clowned around a bit, the first gravedigger has found a skull in the grave – which is a reminder that, in medieval times, it was common to bury people on top of one another, after what you might call a decent period of time – in fact, the gravedigger finds several skulls. He and Hamlet have a conversation about mortality and decay and the gravedigger has some more funny lines and hands Hamlet a skull that he knows to be that of Yorrick, the court jester, whose body has been in the grave for 20 years or so. And that allows Hamlet to say 'alas, poor Yorrick. I knew him, Horatio,' which is the most famous line in the play apart from: 'To be, or not to be.'

"So we're talking about rehearsal, and we're talking about exploring and developing ideas. And when you're rehearsing a play, then at some point you have to rehearse, for example, this scene with Hamlet and the gravedigger. You have to have Laurence Olivier in the same room as the people playing the gravediggers, even if only for a short time. Obviously he will spend more time rehearsing with Ophelia and with the queen and so on, but at some point he has to rehearse with the gravediggers. Take out the scene, and the play doesn't work as well. Remember the poster of Laurence Olivier's *Hamlet* – what image did they choose? Hamlet with the skull of Yorrick, thinking about mortality. But without the gravedigger and his few lines, that essential scene would not work. No gravediggers, no skull. No 'alas, poor Yorrick.'

"And, moving from the theatre to the army – remember our picture of tanks and squaddies running around on exercises? Well, the army also know that you have to rehearse. They understand that it's never as simple as deciding you will do so-and-so and planning it all out on a map and then expecting it to go swimmingly on the ground. They understand that you have to rehearse a battle with squaddies and tank drivers and a few people who know about squaddying and tank driving, as well as the generals. You have to have a go at it with everybody in kit, and then you'll understand whether it works or not. You know, whether you really can get so many tanks on the road in so much time; whether squaddies can actually cover so much distance over this kind of terrain in these kinds of conditions. Because so much of it depends on the abilities and understanding of the people who are going to actually do whatever it is. But, in my experience, this very rarely happens in business."

Piers looked around the team, and saw that he had their full attention.

"Because the people who have a unique understanding of the practical issues involved in the activities of that business," he continued, "don't ever get in the room with the people who make the decisions, for status reasons. I mean, everybody knows this about organizations: if you want to find out how to fix something that's not working, you ask right down at the bottom, they'll tell you what the problem is. Like, 'this part never arrives in time, so we are always held up'; 'this machine only actually works for 80% of the time and then we have to fix it'; 'we could do it faster, but we have to follow this procedure that some bright spark thought was essential, and that delays us.' But the reality is that they never get heard, or they're too nervous to say, or that's not the kind of thing the boss likes to hear. I walk into most business meetings, and everyone is Hamlet. You see what I mean? Everybody who is there, trying to fix the problem, is a leading player – you know, highly gifted and all that, absolutely wonderful – but if you are really going to rehearse something, you need the bloody gravediggers in the room at some point as well as all of the Hamlets; the squaddies and tank drivers as well as the generals; the hospital cleaners together with the finance director."

"Right," concluded Piers. "Time for my last point before we do a couple more exercises. I know you love the exercises!"

Some of the team looked less than enthusiastic.

"Do you know, many of the great ensemble directors might spend as much as half of the time available to put together a performance in exercises to get the group aligned? We explore how we connect; we find rapport; 'being there' for others becomes as natural as breathing. Exercises that used to take an hour are rattled through in minutes. As we bond as an ensemble, we tune in to one another. The exercises are just like a warm-up. And when an ensemble is really in tune, it's almost magical to watch. It's as if they have telepathy. A tiny gesture or grunt is enough to set people off on a path that explores all the possibilities of a particular situation. Ideas become common property and every idea is immediately explored and transcended.

"What I am saying is, don't turn your noses up at the exercises. A group of people thrown together is not an ensemble; it's not even a team. A group of people who have done stuff together and learned to trust one another and are fully committed to doing whatever it is that they have to do as well as possible, without worrying about ego, or status, or embarrassment – that's an ensemble. That's a team. It doesn't happen instantaneously, or without effort. I'm often surprised in business when people complain that a team has been put on a project, and it's not working out. They're not getting the results. Well, that's because you have to work quite hard at making a team, at creating an ensemble, before you can do any good work together.

"Ok! The last idea for the day before the exercises. And it's one that brings together all the other ideas." Piers brought a new image onto the screen: a picture of the serving staff at a well-known fast-food outlet that serves sandwiches, light meals and drinks.

"Have you been to one of these?" asked Piers.

Most people nodded in agreement.

"You walk in and you join a queue," continued Piers "and before you reach the end of the queue, a server who is free is shouting, 'Anybody waiting? Hi – hi: over here! What can I get you?!' And they're all smiling and energized and their mission in life seems to be to make sure to get you served as soon as possible and to make sure that you've got everything you want as fast as they can possibly give it to you and to be certain that you are happy. And they seem to be able to keep that up all day.

"Now THAT is a great performance," says Piers. "That show is going to run and run for as long as they can keep that energy level going. It's working. It's making the punters happy. People come to the show and they love it! They go away and tell other people about it.

"It seems to me that everything that we do in business these days is like a performance. I know you guys make things. You're in manufacturing. You're not a service industry. But I would argue that, although the products *matter,* of course they do – you know, I want a well-made and tasty sandwich; I want a brilliantly designed and beautifully engineered widget – but that is really only the starting point. The way in which I experience your company starts with a good product but needs to transcend that: as I said this morning, business is more about relationships than products, in my opinion. About experiences; pleasures; reassurance. What you guys are doing, I would argue, is less about making and selling products and more about creating ideas and giving performances. What do you think?" Piers looked around at the team, who looked both mesmerized and slightly anxious.

"So the question you could probably usefully ask yourselves is: 'How good is your performance?' I don't mean – I *really* don't mean – how were your last quarterly results, I mean, 'is your audience loving the show? Are you bringing the house down? Is everyone coming back for more?'"

The team exchanged glances.

"So, in conclusion," said Piers brightly. "I have posed five questions, which I hope are useful questions for you to ask about your own organization. The questions are …

"First. Where is our theatre of operation? Where is the place where the real action takes place? Where's the bit of our organization that everyone knows really matters?

"Second. What play are we in? Terribly important. What is the title of the play? What's it about? And what roles are we playing? Sometimes it might be a leading role, and sometimes it's a supporting role. You have to play them differently.

"Third. Do we rehearse and are we a true ensemble? Do we really take part in a co-creative process; do we invite new ideas and allow them to be explored? And are we really an ensemble – do we have that mutual trust, do we feel like we are all in this together and are we determined to make it work?

"Fourth. Are all of the right people in the room for whatever it is we're rehearsing? Or have we got a room full of Hamlets and no gravediggers?

"Fifth. Are we delivering a great performance? Is everything that we do brilliant, especially in our main theatre of operation? Is the audience loving it, and if not, what can we do about it?"

Piers looked at the group.

"Ok, we're just about done for the day. Just one last exercise. We need some more bodies for this one, so let's invite our friends back in."

He opened the door and ushered in the business school staff who had joined them in the morning. Strangely, the board found themselves greeting the newcomers quite warmly. The morning's shared experience seemed to have made them into something of a team.

"Can I ask you to move all of the chairs away? Any way you like!"

"Thank you," said Piers, when an area had been cleared. "Now, could you all please sit on the floor in a circle? I can assure you that the floor is very clean!"

John and Margaret sat down willingly and looked as if they were prepared for anything. Andrew and Rory got to the floor rather stiffly; their faces making it plain this was rather beneath their dignity but that they were going to go along with it for the sake of the workshop. Roger got down to the floor a little creakily and arranged his legs beneath him, looking uncomfortable and unhappy.

"What we're going to do now is quite unusual," said Piers. "Can I ask you to close your eyes, and then, as a group, to count from one to 30, one after the other, but in no particular order. Someone needs to start with 'one', then somebody else – it doesn't matter who – will give us a 'two' – but if two people speak at once, we have to go back to the beginning. You're not allowed to go round the circle taking turns, but that's the only rule. The object of the game is to get to a count of 30 without crashing. Close your eyes please. Let's go."

No one said anything for a while, then one of the school staff said 'one'. After a pause of a couple of seconds, Margaret said, 'two.' A similar pause, and Roger and a female member of the school staff said 'three' at the same time. There was some laughter and a little snort of annoyance from Roger.

"Again please," said Piers.

They started to count again, with a little flurry of successful counts that took them to six, and then there was a pause. The pause lengthened. People became nervous about saying anything in case they clashed with someone else. A brave soul said 'seven'. A pause. Roger and Rory simultaneously said 'eight'. There was more laughter and everyone opened their eyes.

The group tried several more times without getting beyond 'ten.'

"Try to relax," said Piers. "Clear your minds. Just focus on the task."

They tried again.

"How do you feel that last attempt went?" Piers asked.

"I thought we got into a kind of pattern," said Rory. "I thought it was on a count of four, and then if you get in quickly before anyone else..." he trailed off, realizing that this 'system' existed only in his own mind.

Piers turned to Gibbon. "Andrew?"

"Well, we crashed again, but I was beginning to find it quite relaxing!" said Andrew. "It's a bit like I imagine meditation to be. I was starting to enjoy it!"

Several people laughed and made little noises of agreement.

"Let's try again," said Piers.

After a few more attempts, the mood in the room seemed to change. Everyone focused intently on listening; concentrating on the slightest sound from their neighbours in the circle. The numbers were called with more confidence, in stronger voices. The pauses became longer and a curious kind of rhythm emerged, though not one with regular intervals between each spoken number. After several minutes, the group reached the number '30' and spontaneously broke into a round of applause.

"Well done!" said Piers. "Although it may seem odd to you, that exercise is all about allowing space for others: allowing them to use the space rather than feeling compelled to fill the gap yourself. It's about focusing very intently on the others, in this case, through sound. In an ensemble, people become acutely aware of the actions of the other members. If we were to do this exercise every day for a few days, you would get faster and faster. It becomes like one of those 'warm-up' exercise I talked about earlier.

"And that, ladies and gentlemen," concluded Piers, "brings us to the end of this session."

"Thanks everyone," said Mark. "Can we say thank you to Piers?" Everyone applauded. "Now if we can just head back to our own room, I'd just like to do a round-up of the day and tell you a bit about what we have coming up tomorrow.

The delegates said goodbye to Piers and to the business school staff who had joined them in the exercise, and followed Mark out of the room.

"That was good day's work, thank you," said Mark when they had settled back in the room where they had first met in the morning.

"You might like to think about that counting exercise in terms of the jazz we heard earlier. It's not simply a team-building exercise – though it is that – it's also about offering a space to other people and them feeling that they have the right to use that space; about allowing people to make their contribution. Now, can I ask for your thoughts about today? Was there anything in particular that made an impact on you, or struck you as interesting?"

The team looked thoughtful. John responded first.

"I was very interested in what Piers was saying about rehearsal, and about not shooting down new ideas. He's right; we are very confrontational about new ideas and we expect them to be perfect. I liked the notion of half-baked ideas needing to be baked. Also the idea of 'getting the right people in the room' – you know, 'why aren't the gravediggers at the rehearsal?' That's an interesting point."

"I agree," said Rory. "And I'm still thinking about the 'theatre of operations' and about where our 'beating heart' is. Also about whether we practice or rehearse, and whether we rehearse properly at all. That was interesting."

"The whole thing about status was a bit disturbing," said Margaret. "I mean, it's true that status gets in the way of good teamwork and communication – but it's so engrained! I'm sure we send out all kinds of signals to our colleagues that we're not even aware of, and they're probably a bit off-putting. I'm afraid that our colleagues see us as distant and a bit forbidding."

"I enjoyed the jazz session," said Andrew. "I was amazed at how they could play together so well, without even having played together before. And they were able to make up a piece of music out of nowhere, and it was great! I mean, if we could work together like that, we'd be laughing."

"That's true," agreed Rory. "We have teams of people who struggle to work together successfully after years of working together, and yet those guys can get up and perform out of nowhere."

"The other thing that got me about them," said Andrew, "was how much they enjoyed what they were doing. They were having a lot of fun – and that comes out in the music, somehow. I wish our people could have as much fun when they are working together. I wish *we* could have as much fun!" He looked around at his colleagues, smiling.

"And that reminds me about the whole idea of 'performance,'" said John. "You know, 'What play are we in?' 'What's the name of the show?' 'Are we performing it brilliantly?'"

"And the whole issue of ego with the jazz musicians," said Margaret. "You bring a group of musicians together, all at the top of their game, but they don't all jostle for position, they just work together to deliver a great performance. I'm afraid if you brought a group of business people together on a project, you wouldn't necessarily see the same thing!"

"I'm afraid I can vouch for that, Margaret, from my consultancy work!" said Mark. "Everyone wants to solve the problem, but they're possibly more concerned about covering their own backs and, if possible, being the hero of the day – preferably at everybody else's expense! In the performing arts, it's the reverse of that – it's literally impossible to succeed at the expense of your fellow performers."

Mark turned to Roger. "Roger, you're very quiet. Did anything stand out today for you?" Roger looked uncomfortable. "We're all friends here, Roger," said Mark. "Tell us what's on your mind."

"I'm afraid I'm struggling with the whole thing," said Roger finally. "We've got a major issue at work and, interesting though some of this stuff is, I don't see how it's going to help us solve our problem. We were hoping to be able to get your views on some of the issues, but instead we're doing a bunch of crazy exercises."

Margaret started to speak, but Mark stepped in.

"Bear with us, please," said Mark. "This is not a consultancy process. We aren't here to do the usual kind of problem solving – you know: let's analyze the business processes involved and apply the latest techniques to make them all work better. This is about changing the way you think and behave. It's about you exploring all of these different experiences – some of which may well seem pretty crazy! – to see what happens to you. Because, in my long experience, something, at some point *will* happen to you, and it will change your whole outlook. And that's far more valuable than any number of business tricks and fixes that I could suggest for you. We will, by all means, see what light we can bring to bear on your current situation, but we can only do that towards the end of the session, when we've got some new materials to work with. Is that ok?"

Roger nodded, unsmiling. John said, "Of course, Mark, and thank you. We're all signed up!" The rest of the team made little gestures of assent, with varying degrees of enthusiasm.

"Great," said Mark. "Tomorrow morning, we're going to a dance studio not far from the school to see two world-class ballroom dancers called Gunnar Gunnarsson and Marika Doshoris. You may remember my guilty secret was that I danced competitively in Latin American dance for 20 years or so and, in my opinion, these two could go all the way to the top. There's a great deal to be learned from the way that top competitive dancers work together to create winning performances; I think you'll find it very interesting.

"Thank you all. Let's call it a day. I've arranged for us all to go off campus to a nearby restaurant for supper. Shall we all meet at the bar at 7.30?"

The team thanked Mark and left the room, most of them checking their phones for messages as they walked to their rooms.

[1] Keith Johnstone, *Impro: Improvisation and the theatre,* Faber and Faber Ltd, London, 1979

Perform to Win

- Most organizations have a key theatre of operation, the 'beating heart' of their operation; the people closest to that theatre are most significant to the organization's success, regardless of their seniority.

- It is useful to think about what play we are in and what role we are currently playing; true authenticity comes from playing each role appropriately and well.

- All ideas are half-baked at first and need baking; ensembles gratefully accept new ideas and explore them.

- Rehearsal is not the same as practice. Rehearsal is a process of creative collaboration in which things are enacted to see if they work and new ideas are played with.

- Theatres cannot rehearse with a room full of Hamlets – the rest of the cast must be present at some point. Getting the right people in the room is essential for genuine rehearsal.

- Properly functional teams need to be created, like real ensembles; this takes time, effort, commitment and mutual trust.

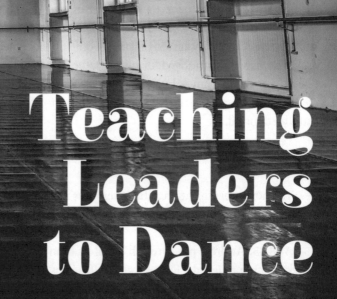

Teaching
Leaders
to Dance

Later that evening, Rory, Andrew and Margaret were chatting with Mark at the small bar near the conservatory that served as the business school's dining room when John approached them, looking flustered.

"I've just had a text from Roger," he told them. "He's left. He says he thinks he should be back at the office tomorrow and he's on his way to the station."

The team looked shocked.

"Perhaps we shouldn't have come just now," said Margaret. "I feel as if this is my fault."

"This is not your fault at all," said John firmly. "You go to the restaurant without me. I'm going to get a taxi to the station to see if I can catch him. I'll try calling him again; he didn't pick up just now."

"I'll call a taxi for you," said Mark. "You head for reception and they'll collect you from there."

John walked off briskly towards reception, re-dialing Roger's number on his phone as he did so. The team exchanged a few words as Mark called for the taxi. They all chatted briefly while they finished their drinks, agreeing to postpone the trip to the restaurant.

"I think I'll head back to my room, if you don't mind," said Andrew. "My guys have sent over some spreadsheets I'd like to look at." Margaret and Rory agreed that they would do the same, and Mark said that he would arranged for supper to be sent to their rooms.

"If you hear from John or Roger, I'd be grateful if you could let me know," said Mark. The group broke up for the evening in a subdued mood.

* * *

The next morning at breakfast there was no sign of either Roger or John. The group sat together at breakfast with Mark. Nobody had much to say.

At 8.45, Andrew put through a call to John's room, and came back looking relieved. "John says he will see us at 9.00 in the conference room," he reported. "He says Roger will be there too." At

9.00 precisely, Roger and John joined their colleagues and Mark in the smaller conference room.

"Good morning everyone," said John. "Roger has something he would like to say and he didn't want to do it over the breakfast table."

Roger stood up very straight, rather like a soldier addressing a superior officer. "I'd like to make an apology to everyone," he said. "I want to thank John for coming after me and bringing me back, but also for not pulling rank. He could have just told me to get my silly arse back here and get on with it."

"Nonsense, Roger," said John.

Roger relaxed his shoulders a little. "John got me on my mobile as I was heading for the station in the taxi and asked me to stop at the nearest pub. Well, he did actually order me to do that, at that point!" John smiled.

"John got a taxi to the pub and we had a beer. We may have had two beers. We may also have gone on to have a curry."

"Which was a very good curry," broke in John, smiling. The mood in the room lifted a little.

"The point is that we talked for a long time about – well, about everything. About the company, about the challenge that we face right now, about what we're hoping to achieve with this programme and what that might do for us. And the point is that I was wrong, and I want to apologize. I really am not comfortable with some of the stuff we did yesterday, but that's no excuse. I'm comfortable with being on an assault course, freezing cold, wet and up to my whatsits in mud and being shot at with live ammo, but I'm not comfortable trying to do acting exercises. I'm not comfortable pretending to be the nine of spades or running around in imaginary thunderstorms picking up chairs. But that's my problem. I don't understand what we're doing here, yet, at the moment, but I should give it the benefit of the doubt."

Roger's colleagues listened intently.

"More importantly," he continued, "you are all doing this too, and we're all in this together. I let the unit down, and that was the one thing I was taught never to do. In fact, in the Royal Marines the punishment for letting the unit down was to be thrown naked into a very large and very prickly gorse bush somewhere on the Brecon Beacons in the middle of the night."

"I don't think they've got any gorse bushes here, Roger," said Mark, smiling.

"I'm glad to hear that Mark, thank you," said Roger. "But I do deserve to be read the riot act and you are all being very indulgent. Thank you. Now, if you will forgive me. I've said my piece and would like to sit down and get on with it."

Roger sat down, with a frown on his face.

"Thank you, Roger," said John.

"So a few beers were had then?" asked Rory, raising an eyebrow quizzically.

"And a few glasses of wine and, possibly, some brandies," said John. "The night porter at the school may have insisted on opening the bar for us when we got back."

"He was very insistent," agreed Roger.

"So we thought we'd have breakfast in our rooms and join you lot together here, rather than to have to face bacon and eggs in public and tell you the whole story then," said John. "And though we are a bit fragile, we are up for whatever you're going to throw at us today, Mark. We're all yours."

"Excellent," said Mark smiling, "because today we are going dancing!"

Roger groaned theatrically and put his head in his hands, then looked up, smiling wanly.

"Do your worst, Mark," he said gamely. "I'm in. 'Lay on, McDuff!'"

"We'll make an actor of you yet!" said Mark. "But first, we're going to make you a dancer."

Roger groaned again, and everyone smiled, though a little apprehensively.

"Let me show you the dancers we're going to meet this morning," said Mark. He selected a file from the conference room's computer and played a short video of two ballroom dancers dancing in the final round of an international dance competition.

When the video finished, Margaret clapped her hands and stared at Mark, wide-eyed.

"They are SO good!" she said.

"They are indeed," agreed Mark.

"If you think you're going to get me to do that Mark…" began Rory.

"You'll have to wait and see," Mark interrupted, smiling.

"We're going to meet these dancers today at a dance studio," said Mark. "They are Gunnar Gunnarsson and Marika Doshoris. I know them both well. They are professionals and they are currently ranked second in England and 19th in the world. They are probably heading for the very top in an incredibly competitive arena. Dance is getting tougher and tougher. It got harder when the Iron Curtain came down, funnily enough, because there was an influx of extremely good dancers from Eastern Europe. Now, a lot of very good dancers from the Far East are joining the international competitions. To get anywhere near the top, you have to be technically perfect – but you also need to have that extra something; that bit of magic. I think these two have that.

"Now if you would, our shuttle bus awaits!"

* * *

The minibus drove the team to a small town nearby. The town centre had the look of an English home counties town from the black and white newsreels of the 1950s. The shop fronts on the high street were built in the Mock Tudor style, with black wooden beams set in white stucco, imitating the oak-framed 'half-timbered' houses of the Elizabethan era.

The dance studio itself had a double front and an impressive, large, stone-framed Tudor-style door with a diamond-paned bay window above. The double doors opened into a reception area with a welcome desk, some chairs and tables and a vending machine full of water and sports drinks.

Mark led the team through another set of double doors on the other side of the reception area. They were surprised to step into a huge space, with a pale wooden floor and mirrors on nearly every wall. The front of the studio backed on to a large warehouse-style building. The room was high-ceilinged and airy. The decoration had switched from Mock Tudor to a kind of Art Deco interpretation, giving the room the feel of a 1920s ballroom with a modern twist.

Waiting for them in the studio were the dancers, Gunnar and Marika.

Gunnar was dressed for rehearsal in black slacks and a dark grey long-sleeved t-shirt. He was in the process of changing his trainers for cuban-heeled dancing shoes.

Gunnar looked like an athlete or a gymnast: tall, slim and broad shouldered. His curly brown hair was worn quite long; he had the bright eyes and well-defined cheekbones of someone who is very fit. The team found it hard to recognize him from the video they had seen. It was not just the absence of Gunnar's flamboyant competition outfits; when competing, with his hair swept back and darkened with hair dressing, he looks like an intense and brooding Spanish flamenco dancer. Off stage, Gunnar was still intense and serious but also approachable and friendly.

If Gunnar was a little different from his professional persona, Marika was almost unrecognizable. When competing, Marika wears a variety of stunning, brightly coloured, figure-hugging dresses and dramatic makeup, all red lips and flashing eyes. As she dances she pouts and poses; dismisses contemptuously or welcomes with a dazzling smile; stamps, spins, leaps and falls with fierce energy and great precision. When she and Gunnar dance together, the air around them seems to crackle and spark.

In person, Marika is petite, quiet and relaxed. Like Gunnar, she is dressed down for rehearsal. She is wearing almost no makeup and her face is soft, pretty and animated. Marika is a French national; Gunnar is Icelandic. They live in the UK and compete for England.

"Ladies and gentleman," said Mark, "let me introduce Gunnar and Marika."

The two dancers smiled at everyone.

"The first thing we're going to ask them to do is to dance a short routine for us."

Marika started a CD playing on the sound system and the two took up position facing each other. They began to dance a rumba. One of the classic Latin dances, the rumba is known as 'the dance of love'. It's about boy meets girl.

Marika placed her hand on the side of Gunnar's face and the two began to dance. Marika snapped to Gunnar's side and they danced some steps together with their hands around each other's shoulders, their movements exaggerated and graceful; they separated and danced slowly around each other, with fluid arm movements. Marika took Gunnar's hand again and twirled beneath his outstretched arm. She spun back into his arms and they moved in tandem to one side.

The couple danced for a minute or so. The effect, at such close quarters, was breath-taking. What looked wonderful on the video looked even more wonderful up close. The dancers' speed, precision, control and grace was plain for all to see; the strength and athleticism required was obvious; the exactness of their coordinated movement was astonishing.

The two finished their routine and the team applauded warmly.

"Marvelous!" said Margaret, her eyes shining.

"Wonderful!" said Andrew.

The dancers smiled their thanks, breathing a little quickly.

"Right," said Mark. "Roger and Margaret, could I ask you to take the floor?"

Roger turned as white as a sheet, but got to his feet and stepped onto the dance floor. Margaret stood up and moved to meet him, looking apprehensive herself; Roger was probably almost exactly twice her weight and eight inches taller.

Mark moved in between the two of them and held out his hand for Roger to shake. As Roger instinctively took Mark's outstretched hand, Mark clapped him on the shoulder and turned to the team: "Can we just acknowledge the fact that Roger thought that I was going to make him dance the rumba, and he was up for it!"

The team applauded, and Gunnar and Marika joined in.

"I am not going to ask you to dance," said Mark.

There was a ripple of relieved laughter.

"What I am going to ask you to do are some exercises that may help to give you a little flavour of what dancers do, and how they work together to create an outstanding performance."

He asked the team to get to their feet, and paired Roger with Andrew, who was closest to him in height, and placed John facing Margaret. Mark himself stood facing Rory and they stood in line together, each facing their partner.

"I want you to put both hands in front of you like this…" – Mark held his hands in front of him at shoulder height, his palms facing outwards – "and rest each other's hands together."

The team joined palms, looking a bit uncomfortable.

"It's interesting," said Mark. "In dance, we touch all of the time. We get quite up close and personal with someone we may hardly know. But in business, we don't touch. We're uncomfortable with it.

"Now, I want all of the people on your side…" – Mark looked at the row opposite – "to lean forward and put your weight onto the three of us until it's uncomfortable for your partner, and us guys…" – he looked to his right at Margaret and Roger – "will signal that point. So, Rory and Margaret, when you begin to feel that your partner is pushing you over, let them know. And then I want the people leaning in to ease off until your partner can still feel your weight, but they're comfortable with it."

The three men leaned their weight onto their partners through their joined hands. As the weight became uncomfortable, their partners let them know and they eased off.

"Ok, do you now feel as if you're in touch with your partner, but not pushing them over?"

The team nodded.

"Now ease off some more so that your hands are still touching but you can't feel your partner's weight at all. At this point, you've lost touch with your partner. You don't know what they're doing; you can't sense what they're going to do next. Now lean back in to the point that you were comfortable with."

The team followed Mark's instructions.

"Now that is what we call the connection. Too much weight and you're being pushed, too little weight, and you don't know where your partner's own weight is. Now try swaying from side to side a bit, still maintaining the connection."

The team swayed from side to side, trying to keep their hands connected with the right degree of weight.

"Now, you guys on that side take a step forward," said Mark, "and we will step backwards. Try to keep the correct weight – the connection."

All the team members suddenly made noises of assent.

"Oh!"

"Aha!"

"Got it?" asked Mark.

"Let's try again with our side leading. Margaret, Roger; feet together. When I say 'go', take a step forward with your right foot, then take a big step to the left with your left foot, and bring your right foot to join the left foot. You guys, step back and to your right and try to stay with us and keep the connection. Go!"

The three pairs stepped forward and to the left, more or less in unison, trying to maintain the right pressure between their joined hands, and stopped with a laugh.

"We're dancing!" laughed Mark. "Well done! But I'm not trying to teach you to dance. We're just trying to experience that sense of feeling enough of the other person's weight to sense what they are doing with their own weight, without being pushed over or losing contact. Did you feel that?"

"Yes!" said Andrew. "It's hard to maintain, but I see what you mean. Goodness knows how you would do that at speed."

"A good point!" agreed Mark. "Margaret, I guess this is familiar to you from your salsa experience?"

"Well I recognize the feeling, in terms of whether you're dancing successfully with a partner or not, but I'd never really thought about it in terms of weight," Margaret replied.

"Please, take a seat again," said Mark, "so that Gunnar and Marika can show us more about 'the connection.'"

"It is largely about body weight," confirmed Gunnar. "And this can quickly become 'push-pull', which is bad."

Gunnar took Marika's hand and led her into a position opposite him on the huge, empty dance floor. They suddenly transformed into dancers again; their bodies held with poise and elegance. Their eyes locked; no words were exchanged but information seemed to pass between them, as if by magic.

They danced a short routine with hands touching. As Gunnar moved forward, Marika glided backwards; as he turned, she followed. With a movement from Gunnar, Marika span to his right on his outstretched arm and was dancing beside him; another signal brought her spinning back to face him. They danced beautifully for a minute or so; it looked effortlessly wonderful. The team looked mystified and applauded loudly.

"Was that part of a routine that you know," asked Rory, "or were you just making it up?"

"I had no idea what he was going to do," said Marika, nodding at Gunnar. "I just followed his lead."

"It's only partly about weight," said Gunnar, "There are parts of any routine where you are not in contact. Let's try this."

They exchanged glances and danced, without touching hands, Gunnar seemed to lead by means of the position and movement of his body: the angle of his hips; a step; a gesture.

When the two dance, they are utterly relaxed in each other's presence and with the physical contact needed for their routines. Like any great partnership, they communicate a great deal without having to say much. Their eyes meet, their hands touch, and complex information seems to be exchanged between them. It is like watching two people telecommunicate.

"This is the partnership I have been looking for," said Gunnar.

"For me too," said Marika.

The exchange is matter of fact; affectionate, but not intimate.

"You can't get the same connection with every partner," said Marika.

"Some dancing partners hate each other," revealed Gunnar.

"Does that work?" asked Margaret, intrigued.

"No!" scoffed Gunnar.

"Sometimes people dance with their real life partner," said Marika, "and that doesn't always work either."

"It seemed that Marika responded directly, following on from what you did with your hips." said John to Gunnar, hesitantly.

"If we are touching, then her movement is initiated by how I shift my weight," said Gunnar, "I can put my spine towards her and lead her into a spin, for example. And if we're not touching then you're right, she responds to what she sees me do."

"Do you always follow Gunnar's lead?" Andrew asked Marika, referring to the established tradition that, in ballroom dancing, men 'lead' and women 'follow'.

"The woman should be constantly active," Marika replied. "You can't just wait for the man's lead; you have to be constantly alert. There probably was a time when it was enough just to follow the man's lead, but times have changed."

"You talked about the connection becoming 'push-pull' when it goes wrong," Mark said to the dancers. "Can I ask you two to show the guys how it looks when the leadership isn't shared successfully, or allowed?"

Gunnar and Marika faced each other and looked into each other's eyes. They began to dance but Gunnar suddenly seemed too strong, too aggressive. Marika tried to follow but the grace of her movements had gone. She looked as if she was being pushed around, which she was. They stopped, grimacing.

"Horrible, eh?" asked Gunnar, smiling now.

"Wow. Yes, horrible," agreed Rory.

"OK," said Mark to the team. "Let's talk about 'looking and see-ing'. In dance, the dancers need to focus on each other as they perform. And it's not a simple thing. Sometimes you might choose to increase your focus on the other person for artistic impact, but you can over-focus."

"It's all part of the connection," said Gunnar. "When you have a good connection, you have a natural focus on each other. You stay in touch all of the time. With some people, the connection is just not there: they dance together, but they're both ignoring each other. It looks wrong. Then some people try to focus too much; they pretend to have focus." Gunnar opened his eyes wide and pushed his face forward in a stare. "It looks forced, stiff."

"Some partners have crazy eyes!" laughed Marika. "They stare at you with these crazy eyes, but they're not really seeing you."

"Let's try a simple exercise," said Mark to the team. "Pair off as we did before, and have a random chat. Establish eye contact – a bit like the exercise with Piers. Then we're going to walk around the dance floor, and I want you to maintain that level of focus, of eye contact, of 'looking and seeing' each other. It's about being present for the other person; about being aware of what they are doing and responding to it, in very simple ways. Let's give it a go."

The six of them paired off again as before, and struck up some small talk, trying to maintain eye contact as Mark had suggested.

"OK, everyone," called Mark, after a few minutes. "How was that?"

"It was quite difficult," agreed Roger. "I mean, I know Andrew very well, and it had never struck me that we don't tend to make that much eye contact. It felt a bit intrusive."

"It wouldn't feel intrusive with your partner, or a very good friend," said Mark. "But we're not very good with colleagues. We look at people, but we don't really see them. We're not really registering what they're thinking and feeling so we're not responding to that, because we can't – we haven't really seen it. Now I'm just going to ask Gunnar and Marika to do us another quick routine, just to see them in action again."

Marika played a new track, and the two danced a samba. The samba is lively, upbeat and fun; it has its origins in Brazil, where they like to party. Gunnar and Marika spun and posed, flounced and stepped, fell into each other's arms and spun away again, looking as sexy as hell. The team were spellbound.

The dancers finished their routine and the team applauded loudly.

Mark asked the team what stood out about the dancers' movements in the last dance. After a slight pause, John plucked up courage.

"Um, hip movement? There was a lot of hip action going on!"

The team laughed, slightly embarrassed.

"Hip movement," agreed Mark. "It pretty much defines Latin American dance. The hips swivel and tilt and sway. Let's try another exercise. On your feet, ladies and gentlemen if you would, and move those hips!"

The five got reluctantly to their feet. To encourage them, Mark performed a few steps himself, very professionally, with some serious hip action. The team burst into applause.

"Respect!" said John, warmly. Margaret clapped her hands together delightedly.

"I told you I could do this stuff!" said Mark, smiling. "So let's give it a go."

The team wiggled their hips, sheepishly, but soon collapsed in fits of giggles and stopped.

"OK," said Mark. "I'm not really being fair. Everyone wiggles their hips when they first try this. But that's not where hip action comes from. Strangely enough, in dance, hip action is not created by using the hips. It's purely based on moving weight from one foot to another. So if you want to create good hip action in dancing, it's not how you use your body but how you use your feet that matters.

"What I want you to do is keep your feet absolutely flat to the floor." The team got into position. "Now transfer your weight completely from one foot to another."

Mark demonstrated, and the team imitated him. Hips began to sway in a surprisingly effective way and the team burst out laughing, amazed. Gunnar and Marika applauded.

"Excellent!" exclaimed Marika.

"Well done," said Mark. "We'll talk about this more this afternoon, because this introduces the concept of input and outputs. In business we tend to focus on outputs, and assume that they tell us all we need. You know, all the usual metrics. But these outputs don't tell us anything about the inputs that created them – human ideas and energy, for example. So the outputs might look ok, but could give you a misleading picture of what's really going on. But, in dancing, you have to start with the inputs, because that's the only thing that will give you the outputs you want. You can't start with the output – like hip action…" Mark swiveled his hips again. "You have to start with the inputs; feet and shifting your weight."

"Does it all start from the feet?" Roger asked.

"For me, it is the feet and the spine," replied Gunnar. "It starts at the top of the body and then works its way down, through the hips, to the legs. Sometimes you might choose to exaggerate the hip movement but it still comes from movement of the spine and feet."

Gunnar talked about how dancers think in terms of opposing forces: to move to the right, for example, they must push to the left.

"I think of it as opposition in all directions," he continued. "I am pushing my weight down into the floor, but also lifting it up through my spine. I can fill up the space on each side with my arm movements, and also behind me and in front of me: now I have balanced forces working in all three dimensions."

"Just a couple more dance-related concepts," said Mark, "and then we can let these wonderful people go." He smiled at Gunnar and Marika.

"The first is about trust," said Mark. "There is a lot of physical risk in high-level ballroom dancing. I've played rugby and done a lot of competitive dance, and the only time I ever got injured was in dancing. Dancers are moving very quickly. In the early stage of competitions, the floor is crowded with other dancers hoping to be picked out to go on to the next round. The woman dancer needs to have complete trust that her partner is not steering her into the path or the elbows of other dancers; when she leaps, she needs to know for certain she will be held; when she drops she has to know that she will be caught. If she has any doubt or hesitation, she will instinctively adopt a defensive position with her body, and that makes it almost certain that she will, in fact, be dropped."

"With a successful partnership, trust is central," said Marika. "With good connection comes absolute trust. I can't dance with somebody I don't trust. I know that Gunnar will catch me. I don't think about it."

Gunnar and Marika locked eyes and seemed to come to a decision. They danced a few steps but Marika called a halt. That was not what she had meant. She demonstrated to Gunnar, folding her body in a drooping position. They danced again and after a few steps Marika folded her body over Gunnar's outstretched arm, with his hand on her stomach. Her body exploded suddenly from concave to convex and she ricocheted away from Gunnar's hand, spinning incredibly quickly across his body. She started to fall, still travelling at high speed, and at the very last second her outstretched hand was caught by Gunnar, who pulled her spinning back up into his arms. The team watched, open-mouthed. Gunnar and Marika stepped back towards them as if nothing remarkable had just happened.

"Final thing," said Mark. "And then we'll head back and talk about how you may be able to relate some of the things we've experienced here to your daily lives. Now, as you may have noticed, Gunnar and Marika are now probably as good, technically, as any dancers in their field anywhere in the world."

The team expressed their complete agreement. Gunnar and Marika smiled diffidently.

"So how do they lift their performance above being technically brilliant," continued Mark, "and introduce the elements of artistry that create a competition-winning performance? Because being technically perfect won't win competitions. There are a lot of other dancers who are technically near-perfect. So how do you introduce something more? How do you introduce some artistry into what you do?"

"Can we just try one last exercise?" Mark asked the team. "It involves walking up and down!"

Mark asked the team to walk from one end of the studio to the other.

"Now walk back to me, but walk differently."

The team started to walk back 'differently' but most came to a halt after a few paces, feeling foolish; looking at each other and shrugging their shoulders. Rory persevered and walked back with a 'silly walk', making huge strides with his feet and holding his arms straight down by his sides. The team applauded.

"Excellent Rory, thank you," said Mark. "Now, it seems difficult when someone says, 'walk differently', but in fact there are all kinds of ways that we can walk. We have names for a lot of them: saunter; slouch; amble; march; stroll; sidle; stride… It's funny how many of them start with an 's'!" Mark noticed suddenly. "But anyway, you see what I mean. So, choose a verb – stroll or saunter or stride or slouch."

The team tried again. Roger marched; no problem there. John ambled, hands in pockets, miming a whistle. Margaret slouched, head down, looking dejected. Rory sauntered, looking chirpy. Andrew strode, crossing the dance floor quickly on his long legs.

"Great stuff," said Mark. "The point is that we can approach even something as simple as walking in different ways. And in terms of carrying out a task, if I can get a bit philosophical about this, we can saunter or we can slouch. Yes? And in terms of performance, we can make something of a 'performance' of it. We can take the basic action – 'walking' – and interpret it in many ways.

"Gunnar, could you tell us more about 'technical' and 'artistic'?"

"Of course," said Gunnar. "Twenty years ago, being technically perfect would probably have been enough to win a competition. But over the years, winning dancers have introduced their own little bits of artistry, and the bar keeps getting raised. The music used in competitive dance is becoming slower, which, perhaps surprisingly, makes the dance more demanding. You need to do things with your body to fill out the music. We'll try to demonstrate."

He and Marika danced a moderately slow rumba, and then a slightly slower version. The slower tempo allowed both dancers to add more detail; the end result was more complex.

"So the extra input, those extra movements, are lifting the dance above the ordinary. Rhythm is another thing we use," continued Gunnar. "We can jazz up the dance by stressing different accents."

They danced and he counted, stressing the third beat in each bar: "One and two and *three* and four and," their movements reflecting the chosen accent.

"Dynamics is another thing that adds artistry," said Gunnar. "Light and shade; white notes and dark notes."

The two danced a routine where they moved their bodies more slowly in some passages, though keeping with the beat, and then performed some explosive 'snaps': fast spins and twirls and rapid movements, before going back to slower movements.

"You can over-dance," said Gunnar. "It's over-powered; you blast every step. You're trying too hard; there's too much tension; it's not so enjoyable."

"We also try to make it more human, to tell a story," said Marika. "The rumba for example, is about a boy and a girl. So you can play that all kinds of ways, and when we rehearse we choose a word. It can be an embrace, or a dismissal. It might be unrequited."

"The Paso Doble is always the bullfight," said Gunnar, "but you can play around with that narrative too. The cha-cha and jive and samba communicate through rhythm. They're just fun. They're more flirty; more of a chase."

"At the early stages of a competition," said Marika, "when you're dancing alongside 25 other couples on the dance floor, you're just trying to get the judge's attention, it could be anything that helps you stand out: your costume; your attitude."

"At the final level of competitions, you need to convey what you are, your unique personality," Gunnar added. "It's about clarity. Make sure what you're selling is clear, consistent and readable."

"Is there anything you'd like to ask these two before we say goodbye?" Mark asked, turning to the team.

"You talked about 'the connection," John asked Gunnar and Marika. "Is there any special technique?"

"We spend a great deal of time together – we practice five or six days a week," replied Gunnar. "In the day we do slow practice; we work on the detail; really small things to improve the quality of the dance. Then we rehearse the whole routine."

"To get to the highest levels," added Marika, "you have to take risks. You have to try something different. That element of risk-taking helps to forge a connection."

"We keep checking on the delivery of every aspect of the routine," agreed Gunnar. "Timing, posture, dynamics, rhythm. We keep thinking about what could be different; what could be better. With dance, there are always new people coming in; they keep challenging you; it makes sure you don't fall behind."

Gunnar and Marika shook hands with the delegates, said goodbye to Mark, and the team left the studio, walking out into the sunlit, suburban high street.

Spending a privileged hour at close quarters with two performers at the peak of their powers had heightened everyone's senses, bringing everything into sharper focus. Something of the passion, energy and commitment of the dancers had rubbed off on them. They felt inspired. The board members laughed and chatted excitedly as they headed back to the minibus, the anxieties of the morning, and of the previous week, temporarily forgotten.

John turned to Rory.

"Where is the *art* in what we do, eh, Rory?" he said, almost to himself. "We are technically good, even brilliant, but where is the artistry? What makes us special? What makes us stand out? That's one hell of a question." He shook his head thoughtfully, and they walked on to the minibus in silence.

Perform to Win

- A winning performance depends on the quality of the connection between the performers. Good connection allows intuitive understanding of the other performers' intentions; it enables masterful performance and improvisation.

- Leadership in connected partnerships is always allowed; leadership based on 'push-pull' does not deliver winning performances.

- Performing artists focus on the inputs that create winning inputs.

- Absolute trust between performers, in the context of the performance, is essential.

- All top competitors are highly proficient technically; elements of artistry make winning performances stand out.

- Winning performances tell an engaging story; winning performers successfully project their uniqueness clearly and consistently.

The Art
in What
We Do

The team took a quick break and then met for lunch in the conservatory. The morning's buoyant mood stayed with them. Roger's near departure the night before had left them feeling distracted and anxious, but after the inspirational session with the dancers, they felt reinvigorated; as if they had weathered a storm together and emerged unscathed and united.

After lunch, they strolled again in the parklands and Roger joined them. They chatted comfortably as they strolled along the pathways, down to the river and back up to the great house. Then they returned to the smaller conference room for the afternoon session with Mark.

"So did you enjoy the dance session?" asked Mark.

There was an enthusiastic chorus of assent.

"What were the best bits? What made the most impression on you? Andrew?"

"Well, I've not been a big fan of dance and I'm a terrible dancer, but just being in the same room as those two and watching them dance at such close quarters… I was just overwhelmed."

His colleagues nodded in agreement.

"It was just uplifting and inspiring and not like anything I've experienced before," Andrew continued warmly. "But also, some of the specific things that were demonstrated really have stuck with me. The connection, for example. I really did 'feel' the point about the other person's weight when I was doing the exercise with Roger." Andrew looked across at Roger, who nodded. "So that was a little insight. And watching the two of them dance so well without any planning or preparation – when they showed that Marika could just sense what Gunnar wanted her to do and where she should go, that was amazing. It was a bit like the jazz band and their improvised piece. It makes me think, 'how can people do something so wonderful without careful planning and preparation? Before we can do anything, we tend to need weeks of planning and preparing. These guys just go, 'let's do a little dance for you that we're going to make up on the spot.' And it's terrific!"

Roger picked up the point. "Yes. It was that amazing rapport. You sensed they were absolutely in tune with each other. I mean, a couple of times they seemed to decide what they were going to do, but they didn't actually say anything! It was just..." – Roger mimed the dancers looking at each other intently – "and then they were off! And the whole issue of trust really struck home. It reminded me of my time with the Marines. It's a big thing that you trust your unit to do whatever it takes if you get into trouble, and you just know that you will do whatever it takes if they get into trouble. It doesn't work otherwise. And that's what Marika was saying. 'I just trust him completely.' I'm not sure we're so good at that in business." He looked thoughtful.

"Thank you, Roger," said Mark. "John?"

"I'm still reeling a bit! I mean, 'where is the art in what we do? How do we rise above what's technically good and make it brilliant?' I'm still turning that over in my mind. I don't know what we can do about it yet, but it just hit home to me. It feels terribly significant."

"Margaret?" asked Mark.

"I'm going straight back to salsa classes as soon as I get home!" she replied. "I loved it! But, seriously – I agree with all of my colleagues. It was very special. I was especially struck by your 'inputs and outputs' idea, Mark. You know, the little bit of dance that I've done means that I should know about that; I kind of know that a good dance move starts somewhere else – with what your feet are doing, or your head, or whatever. But I hadn't thought about that in terms of business. It's absolutely true, we're all obsessed with outputs. That's what the clients and the shareholders and the market want, and that's what we give them and it's essential but you just get obsessed by it. And we measure everything and everyone, not just the business but the people, with appraisals and assessments. And I am responsible for that but I'm sometimes uncomfortable with it. It's as if something or someone doesn't have any value or meaning if we can't put a number on it, and that's not true. So thinking about the inputs that go into what makes our business actually work and produce all of the outputs is very interesting for me."

"Thank you, Margaret," said Mark, turning to Campbell. "Rory?"

"I must admit, it was an eye opener for me. I'm an engineer, you know? If we have a problem, we find a solution. And I can show you what the solution is – I can show you the figures, and build you a prototype and demonstrate that it works. We don't do 'artistic', we only do 'technical'. That's who we are; that's what we do. So to watch something like that and think, 'well, that's not just clever, or technically precise or whatever, that's also amazingly wonderful and beautiful... Am I making any sense?"

"You are, Rory," Margaret reassured him.

"John and I talked about this on the way home," continued Rory. "Where is the art in what we do?' And it's a great question, because there *is* art in what we do. As engineers, you like a beautiful solution. You like something that's elegant. But we don't tend to put a priority on that in business. It's 'does it work?' But 'does it work beautifully?' is maybe a better question."

"Or maybe, from a competitive dance perspective, is it a winning solution?" said Mark. "Because what's beautiful is not just beautiful, it's outstanding. It's what wins competitions."

"Good point," agreed Rory.

"Well thank you very much," says Mark. "Now, if I may, I'm just going to give you my own thoughts about the ideas that we touched on this morning, and then I'd like to shut up..." – Mark smiled – "and give you a little task to do for the rest of the afternoon that will help us begin to use some of these concepts in a practical way. The first thing we looked at this morning, which is absolutely fundamental," said Mark, "was 'the connection'. In dancing, that's the core of it. Because the only way two people can dance together properly is when they have the right connection. And that goes back to Piers's idea about trust and ensemble work – his point that you don't have to like someone to be able to give them absolute trust in the particular context of 'we're all committed to making this particular project work as well as we can.' Simple as that. And in dance, you don't have to be that close to your partner personally to have a great connection. As Marika said, some people dance with their real-life partner, and it can be good, but it's not guaranteed. You might dance better with someone you have no romantic feeling for, but you do have a great connection with. You can just work together brilliantly. And that's what we need in business. You know, romances can be really disruptive in the office. We don't want romance, but we do want a great connection."

The team smiled.

"That brings me to 'looking and seeing,'" continued Mark. "The kind of special focus that great dancers have that lets them stay in touch with their partner even when they're not physically touching. This reminds me very much of what the great theatrical voice coach, Patsy Rodenberg, says in her book *The Second Circle*. I don't know if you've read it? Rodenberg has supplied voice training for some of the most famous actors in the world for several decades. She has been head of voice at the UK's Guildhall School of Music and Drama for 26 years. She also worked for many years at the Royal Shakespeare Company and at the Royal National Theatre. She has worked with pretty much any famous actor you can name and she is a brilliant speaker. She has done some wonderful sessions on development programmes of mine.

"I'm just going to put some slides on the screen," continued Mark, "because Rodenberg defines this better herself. It's the idea of the 'Second Circle' – an ideal state of being-in-the-world, if you like – that she contrasts with the First and Third Circles."

Mark put up a slide.

First Circle: The Circle of Self and Withdrawal
Here, your whole focus is inward. The energy you generate falls back into you. First Circle absorbs other people's energy and draws all outward stimulus inward. When in First Circle, you are not very observant or perceptive about people or objects outside yourself. They interest you only as a means to clarify yourself, not the world around you.

"I do think we can all recognize that," said Mark. "There are some people – or maybe it's better to say that we can all be a bit like this some of the time, and some people are like it all of the time! It's people who suck energy into themselves from the outside world. Everything is about them. It's 'me! me! me!', in a very inward-looking sense. They're not very observant about, or engaged in, the outside world, and if they are, it's because it has something to do with them, not the other person.

"Now, according to Rodenberg, the *third circle* is kind of the reverse of that."

Mark put up the next slide.

Third Circle: The Circle of Bluff and Force
In Third Circle, all of your energy is outward-moving and non-specific, and is untargeted. It is as if you are spraying your energy out to the world with an aerosol can. Your attention is outside yourself, yet unfocused, lacking precision and detail. You get a loose connection to any situation, bit miss the nuances. The world is a dimly lit audience for whom you are performing.

"I think we can all relate to that, too," said Mark. "And, again, we all do it from time to time. I like the bit about 'spraying energy out to the world with an aerosol can'. You know, you've got a script, you've got an agenda, and the world is going to hear about it whether they like or not. It's a kind of bravura performance. It can be impressive, and a lot of leaders behave like this all of the time, but they are not engaging with anybody. It's all a kind of performance but it's the wrong kind of performance: a kind of grandstanding where you ignore everyone else in the ensemble and just stand at the front of the stage and blast away.

"Now, the Second Circle…"

Mark put up the final slide.

Second Circle: The Energy of Connecting
In Second Circle, your energy is focussed. It moves out toward

the object of your attention, touches it, and then receives energy back from it. You are living in a two-way street – you give to and are responsive with that energy, reacting and communicating freely. You are in the moment – in the so-called 'zone' – and moment to moment you give and take [...] In Second Circle, you touch and influence another person rather than impress or impose your will on them. You influence them by allowing them to influence you.[2]

"Performing artists are always in the Second Circle," said Mark. "Gunnar and Marika – we saw that today. When they dance, they have an intense focus on each other. What did Marika say? 'You have to be constantly alert.' That's a good way of putting it. You carefully observe the other person and you make the appropriate response moment by moment.

"How often do we really do that? Be honest!" Mark looked around the group.

"Even with our wives and husbands. You know, you're listening, but you're not really listening. You're a bit distracted. You're a bit back in first circle. And then you think of something important that happened to you today and you move into third circle and sound off for ten minutes and then you ignore whatever your part-ner says in response. I'm not talking about myself here, obviously!"

The team laughed uneasily.

"But in business, how often are we really in the Second Circle?" asked Mark. "Performing artists, every one of them, are always in the Second Circle when they're performing. If not, their perfor-mance will fail. Performance is all about having an exquisite aware-ness of what your partner, or the rest of the ensemble, are doing, and making your unique contribution to that. Doing something that responds perfectly to what they have just done.

"That leads me on to something else we saw this morning, which is the idea of 'allowed leadership'," continued Mark. "Do you remember what it was like when Gunnar was shoving Marika around, when the connection turned into 'push'?" asked Mark.

"Yes," agreed Rory. "Suddenly it all looked horrible! And it was a subtle thing. I don't think I would have thought about it if I hadn't seen them dancing before. But when you'd seen them dancing so wonderfully, suddenly it looked all wrong."

"It is a subtle thing," agreed Mark, "but, again, we do it all the time. In dance, the convention – and it is just a convention – is that the man leads and the woman follows. That's just how it works. Someone has to lead. And in business, I would say, it's the same. Someone has to lead. Someone has to be in charge – remember what Piers was saying about 'in charge but not in control'? And the same thing with the jazz band? That's what I'm talking about. We have to have leadership, and we have to have strong leadership. You guys need to be strong leaders."

Mark looked around the team.

"But that leadership needs to be *allowed*. People are, in fact, entirely comfortable with the idea of leadership. Put a group of people into a crisis, and a natural leader will emerge. We are social creatures. We look for group leaders. Sometimes we challenge them, but the idea of leadership per se is not the problem. And leadership works wonderfully when it is allowed.

"So a question I just want to leave on the table for you is this: 'Is the leadership in your organization allowed, or is it imposed?' Are people working together, or is anyone pushing the other? Because pushing leads to resentment and resistance. It looks horrible in dance and turns horrible in business. You can't push us towards the goal, we have to allow ourselves to be led towards that goal. Or better still, we need to understand the goal so well that we all help to lead each other to the goal."

The room was quiet.

"I want to wrap up now and get you to explore these ideas together," said Mark. "So I'll rattle through the rest very quickly, just to remind you what they were.

"Margaret, you talked about 'inputs and outputs'. It's a simple thing, but it's really important. Remember the hip action exercise? What drives the output may not be obvious. You can imitate an output – you can move your hips to create an impression of hip action – but what generates real hip action is shifting your weight on your feet in the right way; what makes your arms move in the right way comes from the movements of your body, not from waving your arms around. So, next thought. How are the inputs in your organization? The outputs might look ok, but what is driving them? Is it the right stuff? Is the organization actually moving in the right way?

"Next idea," continued Mark. "Trust. Again, I'm not going to labour it. It's like what Piers said yesterday: you have to have complete trust that what you put out there won't be ridiculed or torn apart. That your colleagues will take what you've offered constructively and work on it and polish it and then hand it on. With Gunnar and Marika, we saw that taken to a different level: when Marika falls, she has absolute faith that Gunnar will catch her. That is what makes for winning performances. Well, in fact, it's the starting point. Nothing even begins to happen until you have trust. How is the level of trust in your organization? I mean real trust; at every level?"

Mark looked around the team again.

"Here's something else that I think is often overlooked in business. It's the whole idea of 'the project'. This works in two ways. First, we should see every kind of change as a project, and put the right team on it and ask the team to see it through and then, possibly, to move on. The other aspect of the project relates to winning dance competitions, for example. It could take years. You compete a lot, and you get lots of feedback, which just informs your next performance. We didn't win today, and that was because of this and this. So now we are on to that; now we work on it. And sometimes you and your partner are not in the same place in terms of ability or commitment or time availability or whatever but if you keep switching partners, you won't get anywhere. Because it takes a long time for a couple to gel and it takes a long time to put together choreography that works for you. And if you're not dancing with someone, you could waste a year trying to find another dance partner and getting back on the floor. Because every dancer still has things they're better or worse at, and some choreography suits others, not you, or vice versa. So if you really believe that your partner has the potential, don't waste time looking for someone better. Business leaders often behave as if the answer is a new team. 'Oh, if only we had different people it would all be wonderful'. Probably not. There may be some bad apples that have to be chucked out of the barrel, but in general, the people will deliver when they understand the project and get the right feedback. Businesses also typically focus on very short-term metrics. The next quarter's figures. That's not what builds great companies. It's a long-term project.

"On that theme," continued Mark. "Just a little word about criticism. Because in the performing arts, people are very robust about criticism. Coaches and partners don't bother to tell you that you are wonderful at something. That's in the bag; move on. What they tell you about is what's not working. And that's entirely positive. Nobody makes a fuss about it. 'You need to work on this because it's not working.' Fine, I'll work on that. In business, surprisingly, egos seem to be more fragile. We're just trying to put on a winning performance! I think the problem is that we tend to make the criticism personal. It's as if you are deficient or a bad person in some way. Whereas, if we all agree that we're trying to create a winning performance, it's not criticism, it's a suggestion: 'that's not really working, let's try it this way.'

"And finally!" said Mark. "The last and maybe most important thing we looked at was 'technical versus artistic.' John and Rory, you both picked up on that.

"In dance, there are probably at least 100 couples around the world who are technically capable of winning the world championship. So, with dancing, as with business and anything else, every year one of 100 couples thinks, 'I'm going to find a way of doing something different without destroying the technique.' You can't run a rod over the technique because you will lose. So you have to add your own spin on it, make your performance stand out because you're doing something different.

"There's lots of ways you can do this in dance. But, in my experience, businesses struggle to understand 'where is the art in what we do?' In competitive markets, most people providing products and services are technically capable. So what increasingly matters is, 'what is the artistry that we are offering in our product?' or, 'how are we selling or delivering our service that is going to take us above the competition?' And not only that, but you have to add more and more levels of artistry to win because what is technically perfect this year, with your added three points of artistry, everyone will have added those points next year. So I've got to find another three points. It's an endless battle."

Mark looked around at the team.

"Businesses are comfortable with the technical mastery, because they can write that in a book and explain how to do it. The problem with artistic capability is that it's harder to write, because you need people to be exploring; you have to try things; you have to experience; you have to play. Remember Piers's exercise bringing chairs out of the rain: 'creative leadership thinks as it works.' Dancers play with things in the same way, and it doesn't always work. So, in practice, what you'll do is to make sure the technique is ok, but then think, 'how can I improve that? And then say, 'let's try it this way'; 'what if I do that, will that make it look or feel better or different?'

"Let's wrap this up," concluded Mark. "What I hope may stick with you is that performing artists think about how to win in ways that go beyond how most businesses think about how to win. Most businesses think about mastering technique, and largely ignore the connections and all the other important things they don't really think about, because they don't have the same language. Businesses understand processes and spreadsheets and numbers. They're not comfortable with things they can't put processes and numbers around. If businesses understood some of these things – such as, 'actually, we don't really have any connection to our staff' – then a lot of problems would be avoided. They're not really understanding the lack of connection because they're not asking the right questions. If you ask dancers, 'are you happy in your partnership?' that's unhelpful, it doesn't matter whether you're happy if you're winning. So the questions you would ask around a dance partnership might be, 'are you, as a couple, able to maintain your connection? Do you have trust? Do you have an ability to look and see with your partner?"'

"All those things that performing artists do, they do because it enables them to win. It's not for fun. And these can help us to win in business too, because business is a human endeavour. But if business ever does realize that it needs to explore these human elements in business, it tends to ask simplistic questions. 'Are our people happy?' 'Are they engaged?' Those questions don't give you useful answers; you need to explore specific dimensions. I leave that thought with you!

"And now, to finish the day, your first 'business' exercise of the programme. We've talked about a lot of things in the past two days, so we're going to have a very conventional 'whiteboard' moment. I want you to call out any one of the concepts that were raised in the sessions and we're going to write them down. I just want us to isolate the ideas, the concepts – like Piers's point about hierarchy and status being deadly to real ensemble work. And then, if you want to tell me about any particular issues you have at work, we can begin to think about how these ideas might help. We'll come back to that tomorrow." The team exchanged glances.

Mark wrote 'hierarchy/status/ensemble' on the board.

"So –what else? And then we'll leave these on the board and complete it tomorrow after we've had our session with Peter Hanke. Because tomorrow, you are each going to conduct a choir!"

The group searched their memories for the ideas that have been discussed. They found themselves surprised by how much ground they have covered; the board began to fill up with ideas.

---

[2] Patsy Rodenberg, *The Second Circle: How to use positive energy for success in every situation*, WW Norton & Co. Inc., New York, NY, 2008 pp 16-20

Perform to Win

- Performers forge strong connections by 'looking and seeing'; being present for their co-performers and reacting in the moment to what they do.

- Winning performers set long-term goals and see setbacks as valuable feedback on the road to success; the short-term results are not the main issue.

- Well-informed criticism is a tool for improvement.

- Adding artistry to technical performance is an ongoing issue; winning performers keep at the cutting edge of technique and constantly add additional elements of artistry.

- Issues such as connection, trust, artistry and equality before the task are central to winning performances, but business currently lacks the language needed to discuss these core issues.

Finding
the Pulse

After the final session of the day, the group reconvened for the postponed trip to the restaurant. Everyone was in high spirits and the evening was a great success.

The following morning, after breakfast, Mark introduced the team to the conductor and choirmaster, Peter Hanke, in the smaller conference room. After the introductions, Hanke took the floor.

Hanke is Danish; tall and sturdily built. His receding hairline and glasses make him look rather like an academic or an intellectual; his easy, confident smile and commanding presence make him seem more like a senior business executive. Hanke is all of these things: he has a distinguished musical career as guest conductor for a number of European choirs and orchestras, and was for some years artistic director at the Centre for Art and Leadership at Copenhagen Business School, where he is currently an external associate professor. Hanke is also the founder and owner of Exart, the business through which he runs his music-based executive educational and leadership development work.

"Good morning," said Peter, smiling at the group. "I am Peter Hanke. I think of myself primarily as a conductor. That is the most important thing in my life; that's what I do. But I have also, for a long time now, been involved in exploring the relationship between the arts and business.

"I'd like to tell you a bit about how I moved from conducting to holding master classes in conducting, and then to working in the business field. Then I'd like to talk about what we are going to do together this afternoon.

"In the early years of my career as a teacher of conducting, I was holding classes at the academy in Copenhagen with a number of organists. And you may know, organists are not necessarily the most extravert and open people! They focus much more on their keyboard and many of them will want to make magic with this one instrument; they are not necessarily comfortable standing up in front of a lot of people. I'm a completely different person, I have no trouble in being the centre of attention!"

Peter smiled at the group, all of whom smiled back.

"So I was carrying out a series of conducting master classes with the organists, using a rehearsal ensemble – a small choir – and a business consultant I know asked me if he could try an experiment and have some business leaders try their hand at conducting. So I went to a quite informal gathering with the rehearsal ensemble and the businessmen and women tried their hand at conducting. And I was very surprised by the outcome. These people could do some pretty good stuff without any real musical knowledge, whereas some of the organists – expert musicians – struggled. That got me thinking about conducting and leadership. After all, conducting is leadership. As simple as that. It's not a metaphor for leadership, it is leadership. So I thought that what conductors do and how they do it might have some relevance – it might be useful to business leaders.

"And that was in the early 1990s, and the whole idea was turning over in my mind until, some 10 or 12 years later, I got a very interesting invitation from the Copenhagen Business School to connect leadership philosophy with the arts. Here was the first real chance to mature this concept. Could we use the ensemble and the leader, the conductor, as a laboratory? If we take the masterclass in conducting and these non-musicians who nevertheless have leadership knowledge, could we find a way to make that merge? It turned out that we could find a way; a very fruitful way.

"Later this morning," Peter continued, "we are going to go to a local church where a small choir will be waiting for us, and we're going to take a sandwich lunch and share that with the choir, because I can assure you that nobody ever lost favour with musicians by bringing them food!"

The group smiled again.

"You are going to take turns at conducting that choir. Before that, we will watch some other conductors performing – because the singers in the choir also happen to be conductors who are working with me on a masterclass, and they and I will do some work together to give you some ideas about conducting, and then we'll do some exercises to warm up. But, actually, there is no real preparation that you need. You will find that your leadership experience takes you a long way towards the ability to conduct a choir and make beautiful music together. We are not saying 'this is a bit like real conducting, and conducting is a bit like leadership'. You really will conduct the choir, and they will respond very sensitively to your gestures and your body language, and the result will be instantly obvious; the feedback will be immediate. In my experience, you will learn more about your leadership style in those few minutes than you have ever learned before. You could employ a leadership psychologist, and he or she would observe you and come back months later and tell you something about yourself. But the choir's singing will tell you within seconds, and you will immediately experience that feedback. I don't mean that the choir will say, 'you are a lot like this or that,' I mean the sound that they make will immediately reveal something about your leadership.

"That may sound a bit scary!" said Peter. "In a way, it is a bit scary, but it is also liberating. Only yesterday I was conducting the same exercise with a group of senior executives from a major financial institution. And there is always the same transparency and very quickly a small diagnosis, an X-ray of leadership preferences, instincts, styles and how they appear in front of a group. And the leaders are very shocked, stunned that we can see something significant and important about this person. So a very common reaction is, 'that's really surprising. Is it so clear, do I stand out that much? Is my way of doing things so transparent and so clear in this situation?' That's a common thing.

"I've thought many times about what enables this to happen, compared with more traditional ways of coaching, and have concluded that it is because you accept the invitation voluntarily. You go into the middle of that experience and the music overwhelms you with its beauty. The music becomes persuasive and seductive, and because you have accepted the invitation to go into the centre, defence mechanisms melt away. The armour's off and you stand out as a person, and there we can see a lot. 'Am I into detail or decisions?' 'Can I keep a good overview and create flow of energy that doesn't slow down musicians' expression?' 'Can I observe and analyze while I decide and not lose pace?' 'Can I listen to all signals, or do I unconsciously select favourites?' These things are instantly revealed. Your personal leadership style can be heard as sound, your ability to create structure and clarity, momentum and nuance of detail or overview will be reflected without a filter.

"Some people try to explain in advance why it isn't going to work. You know, 'I don't know anything about music, I'm unmusical, I don't listen to rhythm, I can't hear tones.' We get all these excuses! But what I like to say in response is 'what you're going to do is new, it's uncertain. Have you ever experienced that in your leadership life?' Of course, you have. Every leader has to enter uncertain territories. So then we can say, 'Ok, let's give it a try. We're here to help you. You are in safe hands, there are no hidden agendas and the best thing that can happen is that you succeed with the exercise.' In any sort of leadership you will have enemies and disagreement around you and you will have to fight your way for something. But not here. So the vulnerability is turned, hopefully, into sensitivity. And when it works – which it always does, sometimes wonderfully, sometimes just a bit; but it will work! – then it is a joyous experience. We make music together, with you leading. It's wonderful!

"I'm just going to give you some ideas, some background concepts," continued Peter. "Because, ultimately this is something that you are going to experience. You may or may not be able to put it into words. You may burst with words you want to express at some point. But in conducting, the leader is the only member of the ensemble who does not make a sound! It's the others, the experts, the singers or the musicians, who make the sound for you. That is their expertise. And your job is to lead and to communicate without words. So we start with a disciplined part: 'Don't talk! Be very communicative without words, and then, ok, now we can talk!'

"So there's this sort of oscillation between reflections where you actually do talk, when you intellectualize what's going on, and the other part you get very focused on is this communication with no words. You will see things and most importantly you will hear things, and your senses are used in a combined way. But it's not words, it's not the normal understanding of intellectual knowledge you share with one another that's important. What's important to me is to emphasize that this type of knowledge is not secondary to the words and to the intellectual parts, it's just as important, at least when you create collaboratively with any group. This *felt* knowledge, this gut understanding, is at least as important as the things that we 'know' and can talk about; maybe more so.

"Sticking with the words for the moment, I am going to talk briefly about three sets of ideas in the context of conducting. The first is about leadership itself, the second is about performance and the third is precisely about conducting as a form of leadership.

"First, leadership. Let me give you a bold statement: 'a leader is a visible boss who listens to employees.' What do you think?"

Peter looked at the group, who looked thoughtful.

"A leader is a visible boss who listens to employees," he repeated. "Does that work for you?

"It's not a bad definition," said Margaret after a pause. "It covers a lot of ground."

"Well, let me elaborate on that," said Peter. "'This visible boss encourages the members of the team to express themselves and governs this activity through visual communication and presence.' How are we doing?"

"I can work with that," agreed John. "Though I think there's more to leadership than that."

"Of course there is," agreed Peter, "but we must never forget the issue of visibility. We hide behind emails and memos and expect information to 'cascade down' some imaginary pyramid. But there is no such thing as an invisible boss. It doesn't work. Even Big Brother – you know, in George Orwell's 1984 – nobody ever gets to actually see Big Brother, but he is always visible; his face on giant hoardings and his voice from the telescreens. We are apes, very clever apes, but we still need to see our leader standing in front of us. We need to 'see who is the boss.' And when we do see our boss, it tells us everything: 'The boss is depressed; things are bad!'; 'The boss is happy; things are good!'; 'The boss looks weak – maybe we need a new boss!' We bosses don't like to think that we display all these things, but we do. People see right through us. So we must work with this transparency. Remember that in the real ensemble you have no enemies. Everyone wants this to work. Openness, curiosity, generosity and courage are inseparable parts of both musical performance and of leadership.

"Now anyone who can inspire themselves can inspire others, I would argue. Yes?"

Peter looked around the group.

"All good leaders are inspirational," he continued. "They have inspired themselves and they can transfer this inspiration to others. It is like a transfer of mood and belief. I transfer my confidence and my belief in my vision of the future to you. It is also a flow of meaning. That meaning may be felt rather than verbally expressed, but there is a narrative to it. In music, this would be reflected in melody and phrasing and the leader's decisions about timing, elegance and phrasing would combine in significant ways to shape the final effect. The inspiring musical director can take the ensemble out of a safe place with an unexpected change of pace and strength to produce a striking and novel outcome, and in the right organizational context – in the context of a real ensemble – this is not provocative or destructive, it actually strengthens the organization's cohesion and increases individual job satisfaction. This intervention, this disruption, has an entirely positive outcome."

John raised a hand. "That's quite a challenging thing to say, Peter. That, actually, introducing change, taking people out of safe places and challenging them, can make an organization stronger. People hate change, in general."

"Well, the proviso was 'in the right organizational context' and 'in a real ensemble,'" replied Peter. "When you are genuinely creating something together then yes, in my opinion, challenge and change can be welcomed. In fact, they are necessary. That is what the leader must do. And people will find it challenging, but also rewarding.

"The one final thing I would say here is that the leader may have the power, but the organization has the force. The job of the leader is to unleash this potential in a focused and targeted way. In conducting, as in leadership, there was an old-fashioned model of the conductor as a dictator, as a despot, demanding obedience from the orchestra or choir. This was always nonsense. The conductor may be demanding; he or she may be very difficult and push the ensemble beyond its comfort zone, but the conductor cannot dictate; they have to earn their status, collaborate and inspire. Without the ensemble, the conductor is just a crazy person waving his arms around!"

The team laughed quietly.

"Let's grab a quick coffee and I will finish my thoughts before we go to the church and actually experience what I am taking about."

The group fetched themselves drinks, and returned to their seats.

"After leadership," resumed Peter, "let's reflect a little on the concept of performance.

"My thinking has always been that the arts bring together many virtues of human endeavour. Artists are concerned with novelty, innovation, excellence in performance, heightened sensibilities. The arts bring together people from many different backgrounds and enable them to work together to produce a beautiful, challenging performance. The arts help us to see new ways of understanding human capabilities; to use more of our own potential and to stimulate growth in other people.

"Now, in modern business, we all talk happily about learning, knowledge, creativity, innovation and performance. All of which are meat and drink to the performing artist, so we should be talking the same language here.

"But in business, the issue of 'perform!' carries something of a threat. You know: 'Perform or else!'"

The team smiled to themselves.

"And the whole of management vocabulary has been hijacked by bottom-line discourse. We need to reclaim the notion of performance. Managers and leaders do in fact, perform, but the language of measurement and the bottom line ignores the complex relation-ship between the manager and their employees. We can't measure that, so we ignore it. But it is vital. Successful leadership can, in fact, lead to beautiful organizations, just as it can lead to beautiful music, or beautiful dance, or beautiful theatre."

"What do you mean by beautiful organizations?" asked Andrew.

"Good question. What do you think? I personally think that our notion of organizational beauty has changed and is probably still changing. For example, in the days of scientific management in the early twentieth century or thereabouts, managers were obsessed with efficiency. 'We have very productive new machines, and new power sources, so we must make people as efficient as the machines.' So, to them, a 'beautiful' organization would be a highly efficient organization. Now, I would argue that people are not machines, and that we need them to be not machine-like, but human, in their work. We need their ideas and creativity and their ability to collaborate and transmit and transmute ideas. For me, I can't imagine a beautiful organization that is not creative or that is not full of people who are happy and fulfilled in their work; who have a sense of common purpose and the sense of satisfaction that derives from achieving a common purpose. For me, a beautiful organization has to be like a happy choir, making joyful music. I mean, is a sweatshop paying minimal wages to make clothing as cheaply as possible for the global market beautiful? Not for me. Is a better-led organization that works together to create afforda-ble clothing with a workforce that feels engaged and involved and where the organization is a force for good in the local community beautiful? Probably yes.

"Good leaders surround themselves with co-players rather than with co-workers. Work is increasingly full of people with special-ized knowledge – and I include people who are specialists in using a sewing machine or specialist machine workers just as much as specialist computing coders or financial experts. We have to har-ness the efforts of the specialists, who are like virtuoso craftsmen and women. It's a lot more like a craft workshop than a factory.

Nothing should be absolutely routine. Nothing does not benefit from aesthetic input."

"Forgive me," interrupted Rory. "Aesthetic?"

"I think so," replied Peter. "A great deal of what the modern worker does is to handle complexity. And to deal with complexity, we use what are essentially aesthetic tools. We use taste, discernment and personal decisions to choose the best route through the various mazes of complexity. This is the absolute converse of 'efficiency': this is using human beings for what they are best at – subtle discernment and the expression of personal taste. How often do we say that a certain solution is 'beautiful' or 'elegant'?"

"Ah well, yes – we talked about that yesterday," agreed Rory. "Even in engineering, some solutions are definitely more beautiful than others. We look for beautiful solutions. But I have begun to wonder what I mean by 'beautiful.'"

"Aesthetics," says Peter. "A subtle judgment, not based on logic or reason, that this is more lovely; more beautiful. When we face a seemingly impossible problem, we allow our 'gut feelings' to tell us what to do. But this is not just 'instinct' because our aesthetic sensibilities can be trained and improved. This is what artists do. This is what leaders and managers can do if they begin to think more like artists."

Peter began to wind up.

"My final set of ideas. This is about conducting, which you are about to experience. Let me give you a very simple description of conducting. Every musical composition has a basic pulse, and the first, the most obvious issue, is which syllables of this pulse should be stressed, and which should not. When conducting, move your hands down with gravity on stressed syllables, and lift your hands on unstressed syllables in accordance with the basic pulse of the composition. There are also phrases that rise and fall in a larger rhythm – expand your gestures to include the energy of these larger phrases. And then there is, of course, an endlessly refined scale of expression in the tension between stressed and unstressed micro events – so this apparent simplicity can become very complex.

"Remember that this is a joint statement between you and the musicians: leave it to them to take care of details. Musicians are perfectly capable of 'keeping time.' They have been trained to do this. This can be seen as the equivalent of 'following the business plan'. It is straightforward. The conductor is there to bend the pulse, to articulate the language so that it becomes more nuanced and doesn't just sound like a machine. The same, I would suggest, with business leaders. You can leave a lot of the detail to the team, and you can trust them to keep the beat, the pulse. What is interesting is the bending of the pulse; the interesting difference."

"In leadership terms, we can see each of the underlined gestures as decisions. Every time a leader strikes a 'beat', he or she has made a selection or a de-selection; a direction has been set or a pace shown; a level of volume and force is indicated. The managerial work is done; a decision is taken. Now we can talk about the quality of the decision, and whether it is appropriate for the musicians to follow it. The core and its relentless pulse calls on the manager and their decision-making power.

"And this brings us to a central point, which is the battle between control and inspiration. If you insist on control, you will deliver no inspiration and get no surprises. To raise the level of inspiration, it is necessary to challenge ruling systems and pre-dictability. This is the subtle difference between motivation and inspiration. You can, they say, motivate people using fear and rewards, and they will work for as long as they are 'motivated' and then stop. But when people are inspired, they work because they want to, it has been internalized.

"Where there is a real symbiosis between ensemble and con-ductor, this creates a shared power, where the conductor as leader can participate fully in the community of musicians. This is a joy-ful state of mind. The reason musicians perform together is to be able to enter into this joyful state. And in this state, hierarchies are irrelevant – there is no difference between the conductor and the ensemble; the musical greatness is owned by all and the power relationship has evaporated."

The team listened intently.

"We're going to go off and experience some of this. We are going to stop talking and start communicating non-verbally. And the final business point is that we all need to think very carefully about our non-verbal communication. Employees today are more aware of the leader's personal signals than ever— even if they see them only on a screen, when the leader appears on the news or at a huge conference. Body language is interpreted and assigned subtle meanings that may go far beyond what it was intended to express, so that contemporary leaders must pay special attention to personal expression and any unintended effects it may have.

"But my final thought is this: the entirely predictable and apparently omnipotent leader is ultimately boring. We know what they are going to try to convey, so who cares? Great leaders are those who dare to play with unpredictable aspects of their personality: to be transparent. When we risk this, we are usually rewarded."

With this Peter wound up the session, and the team collected their packed lunches and headed for the minibus to take them to the conducting sessions.

Perform to Win

- Leadership is embodied; the response to embodied leadership is immediate.

- Our felt knowledge is as important as the things that we 'know'; the most significant elements of communication are non-verbal.

- A leader is a visible boss who listens – who encourages the team members to express themselves and governs through visual communication and presence.

- Leadership intervention, disruption and challenge improve performance and make organizations stronger.

- Leaders have the power, organizations have the force – leaders bend the pulse of the organization and make selections.

- The concept of performance in business has been hijacked by bottom-line discourse.

- Increased complexity demands aesthetic solutions; successful organizations, like elegant solutions, are beautiful.

- Successful and authentic leaders accept the risk that transparency brings; predictable, omnipotent leadership is uninspiring.

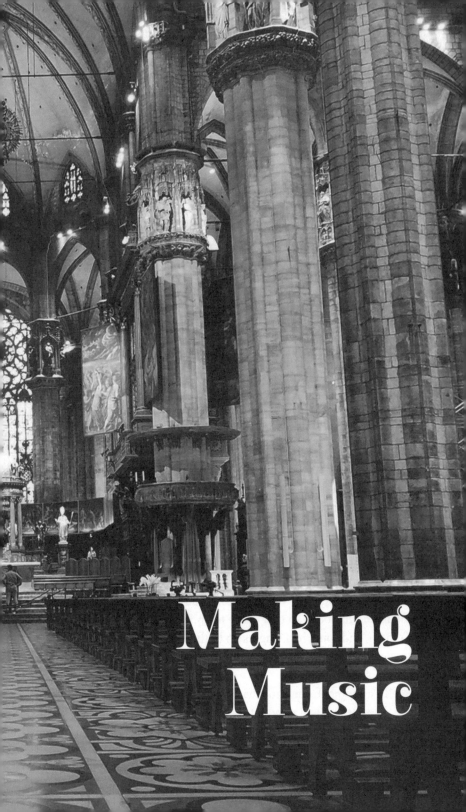

Making
Music

The minibus took the team to the suburbs of a nearby town, a little further down the river. It pulled up in the driveway of the impressive church of St John the Evangelist, built in the classic Victorian gothic style, with lancet windows and a tall spire, visible from miles around. The church was built on a grand scale; inside, the long, high nave had a gallery built up on both sides, supported on cast iron pillars, to accommodate more worshippers. Above the entrance, at the opposite end from the choir and the altar, were the pipes of a large and impressive church organ.

The team went into the church. The high ceiling of the nave towered above them. The walls beneath the galleries at both sides of the nave were decorated with a series of biblical scenes created from hundreds of brightly coloured small mosaic tiles in the Byzantine style much favoured by Victorian architects. Sunlight flooded through the great stained glass windows above the altar; the rich blues, greens, reds and golds of the mosaics glittered dimly on the walls, giving the church an exotic feel, more reminiscent of a Greek Orthodox Church than the typical English church.

Peter led the team down the nave to the vestry, which was filled with a large scrubbed pine table surrounded by chairs. Cupboards lined the walls. The room smelled of dust and hymn books. The four singers were at the table, drinking tea. The team unloaded the packed lunches, which were warmly welcomed by the singers. Peter introduced them – Elizabeth, Justin, Penelope and Michael – to the team.

After lunch, the group moved from the vestry into the main church and sat themselves in a rough crescent around the space where the conductor would stand. The singers took seats among the team members, so that every team member had a singer next to them, and some had singers on both sides.

Peter addressed the group from the focal point of the little crescent of seats.

"In a moment, the choir will sing and you…" – Peter smiled at the delegates – "will conduct them. Now you might imagine that the choir will sing the piece very well, regardless of what you do –

which the choir is entirely capable of doing. Choirs and orchestras are quite capable of ignoring a conductor that they don't like, if they choose to!"

Peter smiled, and the singers laughed.

"But these singers will not do that. They will respond to whatever message your conducting sends out. If you set a slow tempo, they will follow that tempo; if you speed up, they will speed up. More importantly, the choir will respond to every message you send out, consciously or unconsciously. If you are nervous, they will be nervous. If you are joyful, they will be joyful. If you are overbearing, they will be cowed. It is always interesting!

"But first, let's just do some quick exercises. I will ask the choir to join us just so you can have some different partners. Please stand up and find yourself a bit of space, and let's wave our arms around! A lot of what you convey as a conductor comes from your arms and hands – not everything, but a lot – and we northern Europeans tend not to use our arms and hands so much when we communicate. So let's free them up. Let's be expressive with our arms and hands! It doesn't matter what you do, just get them moving around; loosen up your shoulders and your neck."

Peter started to move his arms with bold movements, drawing large imaginary circles with his outstretched hands, shrugging his shoulders one after the other and moving his head to loosen his neck muscles. The team and the singers followed suit.

"Now, please find a partner. There are nine of you here, so I will be someone's partner..." Peter went up to Roger and stood in front of him. "And could the team pair off with a member of the choir. Just take it in turns to mirror each other's movements. One of you make a series of gestures and movements – any movements – and the other one should mirror what they are doing.

"OK, now switch around please, with the other person initiating the movements."

"Thank you. It's interesting. But you may now feel that you know your partner a little better than you did, yes? You haven't said anything, you haven't told each other anything about yourselves, but you may feel that you have some kind of idea of what the other person is like. Now, one final exercise. Could you take it in turns to communicate with each other just with gesture? Don't say anything, just use your arms and hands. It doesn't matter what you are trying to 'say'. You might want to tell a story or just express something. Just communicate, but without words. Could the people who were first in the 'mirror' exercise go first again?"

The pairs started to move their arms. Strange faces were pulled as people strained to express some idea; arms were waved; hands fluttered. After a while, Peter asked them to stop, and most of the 'watchers' said supportive things to their partners.

"I felt that you were trying to describe something to me."

"I sensed that you were telling me a story."

They switched partners and repeated the exercise and then Peter called a halt.

"Excellent. That last exercise is actually more difficult than the conducting, because when you conduct, you have the raw material. You're not trying to make up a story, the story is unfolding in front of you, and you must direct and influence it.

"Now, as I was saying, our singers today are not simply singers. Elizabeth, Penelope, Justin and Michael have been working with me on a conducting masterclass: they are all highly experienced musicians who want to develop their conducting skills. So, with their permission we would like to conduct a short masterclass, so that you can see the kind of issues we work with; the kind of thing that we do as we hone our conducting skills. Then it will be your turn. I will join the choir, so that when one of the class conducts, we still have a four-piece choir for them. But first, we need to rehearse a bit!"

Peter picked up a chair and asked the group to rearrange themselves as he inserted a chair for himself into the semicircle. He asked the singers to turn to a piece of music from the seventeenth century: William Byrd's 'Ave Verum Corpus', written for unaccompanied voices. The singers began to sing. The effect, in the rich acoustics of the empty church, was wonderful. The team, sitting among the singers as they performed, listened entranced.

The singers, however, were not yet happy with their efforts. They ran through it again. There was general agreement that they were performing better together. "That flowed a lot better," said Penelope.

"I'm sorry to interrupt," said Rory, "but what do you mean by 'flow'?"

"Flow is what the conductor is looking for," said Peter. "And indeed the performers. It's a multi-dimensional thing. There is a flow where you perform something and you can feel now it's really one phrase taking the other, lifting it off and it really grows around us, it's a very powerful and happy feeling. That's where we can talk about happiness for performing artists, where one tone just grabs the next and you feel like a medium, you don't do anything, it just goes into that mode. So 'flow' is what we want."

With the singers feeling they were performing well enough as an ensemble, Peter began the masterclass.

Penelope is a professional singer who has moved into conducting and now directs and coaches choirs. She has joined Peter's conducting masterclass to develop her conducting technique.

Penelope took her place in front of the choir for the first conducting exercise. The conductors, Peter included, used their arms and hands only when conducting; batons tend to be used when conducting a full orchestra. She conducted the group, which sang 'Ave Verum Corpus' once more – wonderfully, to the team's ears.

There are certain conventions in the 'language' of conducting – patterns of beats and particular gestures developed to achieve specific technical results – but the many issues of pace, dynamics, accent, volume and so on are expressed via a more general body language: movements may become shorter and sharper in fast, percussive passages; more languid and expressive in the more sweeping, emotional passages. Conductors may signal what is needed by a look, a movement of the head, or even by a visible intake of breath. What the conductor does, physically, when there is a successful bond between the conductor and the players, is miraculously transmuted into sound. The bodily gestures of the conductor create instantly recognizable changes to the music. Their physical expressions translate directly into precisely different outcomes. It is like a kind of magic.

When the piece ended, Peter offered Penelope some suggestions. "Try more horizontal arm movements. At the moment you beat too much and conduct too little. Try lighter beating and more movement; caress the sound."

He stood behind Penelope, took her right hand in his own and conducted with it. The team noticed how intimate this was. In most performing arts, physical connection is not merely acceptable, it is essential. When musicians play or sing together, physical contact is not essential, but players are intimately linked via other senses: they hear and see (and to some extent feel) what the other players are doing. With conducting, it's more physical. As with actors and dancers, the conductors' bodies have become the medium that conveys meaning and emotion. Conductors, actors and dancers develop a more objective approach to their bodies: their modes of physical expression are no longer merely personal to them; what they do with their bodies has a precise and significant impact on their performance and their audience. It is essential that they are aware of this and learn how to put their bodies into the appropriate configurations. As a result, they are very tolerant of others invading their personal space.

Peter encouraged Penelope to be more expansive. "Keep delivering the beat, but more like painting pictures in the air. Hand over the sound to the choir at this point." Peter made an outward gesture with both hands, as if handing something over to someone else. "Give us more participation."

Penelope tried out the new approach. "It feels as if my arms are freer and more connected to the music," she said.

"Breathe together with the singers," suggested Peter, indicating that she should try to harmonize her breathing with patterns of breath dictated by the phrasing of the music.

Penelope restarted the music.

"That's very nice and legato," she said, pleased with the sound her conducting was coaxing from the choir.

"Try it with no hands," suggested Peter. "Just use breathing and head movements!"

Penelope conducted the choir with no hand movements, moving her head expressively and breathing with the choir. It sounded good.

It was Elizabeth's turn. Elizabeth was originally a pianist before studying choral conducting; she is the musical director of two UK-based choirs and a popular guest conductor.

She conducted the group, brilliantly.

"You are such a responsible person," Peter told her. "You deliver the beat. Don't. Free up the ensemble."

He encouraged Elizabeth to be less concerned with the beat – with 'keeping time' – and to convey other ideas to the singers with her gestures.

Elizabeth conducted a few bars, but seemed uncomfortable.

"You don't like it," suggested Peter, "because you are not in control."

"No, that's my thinking face, that's all. I don't not like it," Elizabeth replied, though she seemed put out.

To the team, this looked like a challenging exchange. It was, in fact, challenging, but also entirely positive. Everyone in the masterclass had 'signed up' for this kind of rather personal, slightly challenging analysis of what they do physically when they conduct. Disagreement is allowable; feeling hurt and flouncing off is a waste of everyone's time, and therefore not allowable (unless it quickly passes and is not often repeated: behaviour that is only tolerated in the greatest 'prima donnas'). Comments by coaches or directors can be direct, if it is a question of a wrong technique that must be corrected. Among themselves, however, performing artists tread more carefully on each other's feelings: it is not for them to criticize a fellow performer. Comments tend to be along the lines of: 'What if we try it this way?' 'I'm not sure that quite works; shall we try again?' 'Something seems to be going wrong at this point here.'

It was a remarkable proof of the conductors' robustness that they were happy for a team of strangers to watch them work so openly with Peter. Elizabeth explored her new techniques as she conducted the piece again and Peter asked the singers for their opinion. Justin offered some feedback. "Initially it felt a bit too controlling. It felt tense." He pointed to his throat. "Now it's flowing better."

When the singers gave feedback in this way, they tended, like Justin, to refer to physical sensations, not to intellectual concepts. What the conductor was doing with his or her hands and body was having a direct physical effect on the singers' bodies, affecting the sound that they made. Something about Elizabeth's earlier technique was indeed being experienced as controlling; Justin felt tension in his throat; his singing was affected. Her new gestures had changed this; his throat was more relaxed; his and the other singers' music 'flowed' better.

Now it was time for Justin to conduct.

Justin is a pianist and composer by training and is also musical director of a choir in Singapore.

The choir sang 'Ave Verum Corpus' again. Justin beat time with his right hand, and with his left hand called in voices on their cues, then made a gesture asking for the music to swell.

Peter interrupted. As with Elizabeth, he recommended that Justin worried less about giving the singers the beat. "There is too much beating. It tells the musicians what they already know. It's a sort of non-conversation; it gives orders that are not necessary."

He stood behind Justin, as he had with Elizabeth, and took both Justin's hands to conduct for him. The choir sang. The sound was noticeably less rigid, less defined; more expansive.

"Imagine that you are playing a large cello," suggested Peter. "Sound comes with the movement of the hand, not with a percussive beat."

Justin experimented with this. "We are getting extra movements now," Peter told him, "and it's becoming a bit hard to follow." He made another suggestion: "Imagine that your hands are linked together by a soft rubber band." Peter put both of his hands in front of him, palms vertical and close together, and then moved them apart as if they were indeed linked by a rubber band that prevented them from moving too far away from each other. The movement of his hands was less expansive; more focused. "This idea is to stop either hand doing things that are not important to the sound; it creates smaller movements and keeps the palms connected."

Justin conducted again, exploring the technique; making less dramatic, expansive gestures with his hands and arms.

"That feels more supportive here," Penelope told Justin when the choir stopped singing, pointing to her diaphragm. "That's lovely!"

Michael took his turn to conduct. Michael is the director of a marketing agency but also a choral singer and the director of a choral consort. His gestures when conducting tended to be gentle, vertical movements; occasionally they were more sweeping.

Peter suggested that Michael should move his arms away from his body more, creating space between his arms and the sides of his body. "Give the music to the singers," Peter said again, making a forward gesture with his hands, like someone offering a gift.

Michael tried the new techniques and the choir immediately responded; the sound that they produced was somehow warmer, richer.

"Wonderful!" said Peter. "Freeing up your arms makes you more connected with the sound."

Peter talked about the beat of the music; the pulse. Although he had recommended that the conductors should be less overt in beating time, it was still essential that they had 'an internal click track'; that their sense of the music's pace was the same as the singers.

"It's reassuring when I look up and you're in the same place as my inner pulse," Penelope told Michael. "It's distracting when that's not happening. I feel more connected when they're in harmony."

It was time for a break. The team produced some biscuits that had been supplied with the packed lunches, and were warmly thanked. "You can come again," said Elizabeth.

As everyone drank their tea, the team asked Peter about his own approach to conducting.

"For me, it's all about blending the voices; sometimes allowing one to stand out, but without being isolated. In particular, it's the ability to embody what the singers need. You don't need to be a brilliant singer yourself; you produce your results through others. As a conductor, your uniqueness is more important than the technical brilliance of your hand movements. You need to make a real connection between people. There is also an endless number of things that musicians need from you: you must keep the agreements that are made in the process of rehearsal."

"One thing that interests me," said John, "is that these people are all presumably trying to carve out their individual careers in music: they all obviously want to be the best. But they have no problem singing together to produce great music, or exposing themselves to their peers with you criticizing them – in the nicest possible way, of course!" John smiled at Peter. "But if this was a collection of business executives, there would be a lot more jostling of egos, and people would be putting up barriers. And we tend to avoid that kind of scenario, because it usually ends in tears!" said John. His colleagues all nodded.

"It's like the first and second flute in an orchestra," said Peter. "The second flute aspires to be good enough to become first flute. Everyone aspires to improve. But the music comes first. And a conductor must remember to serve the choir; to move it forward."

The conductors reconvened for a second session to try out Peter's suggested techniques.

Michael conducted the choir in a difficult modern piece, 'Gaudet Mater', composed in 1971 by the Danish composer Per Nørgård and based on a twelfth-century text and melody. Like much great music, it sounds delightfully simple but is technically demanding. The time signature shifts in places from bar to bar. The choir got lost in a few places, and Michael guided them through. "We can see your pulse is really internalized now and that's contagious," said Peter.

Michael found that his new techniques were having an effect. "It feels very different," he told the group. "Freer somehow. I think it's a physical thing."

"It is a physical thing," agreed Peter. "You look up more. You are more connected. Your hands are more connected with the music now."

As each conductor started a piece, he or she smiled confidently and radiantly, raising their chests out of their diaphragms and lifting their heads. The choir unconsciously mirrored their body language, putting them into a buoyant mood and the correct physical posture to sing at their best.

Elizabeth conducted the choir in a particularly beautiful and moving work, 'Locus Iste' by Anton Bruckner. The choir sounded especially rich; the voices blending together so well that the air in the church seemed to pulsate.

"Now the choir likes your help and your guidance," Peter told her. "You have a good connection. Now you can take it further. Float on this energy you have and then launch the big thing. When you have launched, you can just keep that kettle boiling."

"I feel underprepared," said Elizabeth. "I haven't studied the score before today; I don't feel I'm adding anything."

"It's not about errors," said Peter.

Penelope acknowledged the effect that Elizabeth's conducting was having on the group. "I love the sound you're getting from us," she said. "I'm trying to work out how you're doing that. I think it's posture."

"It is posture, and gesture," confirmed Peter. He referred again to using the hands 'as if joined by elastic bands'.

"It feels more connected to here now," said Penelope, pointing to her stomach. "That feels good." Elizabeth smiled happily.

When it was Michael's turn to conduct again, Peter made fine adjustments to the position of Michael's arms, placing them slightly further away from his body with the palms slightly less vertical, more horizontal and open. These small changes resulted in an audible improvement in the sound produced by the choir.

"To increase volume," suggested Peter, "have two different sizes of what you do – a set of more expansive gestures. You're leaning forward here, which is understandable, but you get more effect if you lean back. Leaning forward is quite intense; you feel scrutinized, urged on. The effect of the conductor leaning back is more expansive; liberating."

With Penelope, Peter slightly adjusted the angle of her upper arms, and advised that she made her arm gestures at a lower level, more at waist level than at chest level. The effect was strangely powerful and encouraging; the choir responded. "It's more comfortable," said Penelope. "It takes the strain off the shoulders."

The masterclass came to an end and Penelope returned to her seat among the delegates.

"Now it's your turn," said Peter to the delegates, smiling. "Who's first?"

Rory raised his hand.

"Excellent," said Peter. "A volunteer."

The team murmured their support.

"We're going to try a Bach chorale," said Peter, asking the choir to locate the correct sheet music. Rory raised his arms, and brought them down to start the music. The choir started to sing. Rory had set a slow pace; the music sounded rather laboured and ponderous. The choir diligently followed his lead, but the piece seemed to be getting more and more bogged down.

Peter intervened.

"How is this working?" he asked Rory.

"I'm struggling a bit," said Rory, "but I'm not sure why."

"Can I?" said Peter. Standing behind Rory, he took Rory's right hand and raised it. The choir began on Rory's downbeat and Peter moved Rory's hand in a subtle but precise pattern that brought the choir in at a much brisker tempo.

A look of recognition spread across Rory's face.

"That's more comfortable – for everyone," said Peter. "But now that we've got a better speed, don't worry too much about the beat. Tell the choir how you want them to sound."

Rory started again at something closer to the faster tempo, but now made increasingly dramatic gestures with his arms. The choir began to falter. One singer stopped, then another. The music fell apart and the choir laughed to defuse any tension. Peter quickly stepped in.

"Don't worry! That was too much. That was too expansive; too dramatic. The choir didn't know what you wanted them to do. Make smaller gestures; keep your arms closer to your body. Stay with that pulse that we established and listen to the choir. Just nudge them in the way you want to go. Remember that we need clarity of decision making. Make your decision and communicate it clearly."

Rory started again, making greatly reduced gestures with his arms and hands. He established the pace, and allowed the choir to follow his simpler movements. The choir began to relax and the music began to come into its own. It was obvious to everyone in the team that it was beginning to sound good. Rory's confidence increased, and his body language became subtly more expressive. The sound swelled and became richer in texture. The choir reached the end of the piece and everyone applauded warmly. Rory looked elated.

"Very good!" said Peter. "The choir want to sing; they know the piece. Let them perform and then make your own contribution; guide them in the way you want them to go; make some decisions. Control your arm movements a bit more: remember we talked about imagining that your hands are joined by an elastic band? And also perhaps try to keep your arms a little closer to your body and a little lower. It helps the sound to come from here." Peter patted his stomach. "Let's try a different piece, a part-song by Mendelssohn." Peter nodded to the choir, who changed their sheet music.

Rory started the choir and they sang well for a minute or so before Peter stepped in.

"You are too focused on the detail," Peter suggested to Rory. "You are worrying about every detail. Leave that to the singers. Look for the longer phrases; think about the larger shape of the music. Try to bring that out. Don't tell the choir what to do every second; think about the bigger picture."

Rory started again. His conducting became less directive, more encouraging, the choir instantly responded. At the end of the piece, the last notes reverberated through the church. Rory was visibly moved.

"Well done," said Peter again as Rory took his seat, his colleagues patting him on the arm as he passed and clapping their hands silently to show their appreciation.

"Who's next?" asked Peter.

Andrew stood up and moved to the front. The choir went back to the Bach chorale and Andrew signalled the start. His movements were stiff and precise. He looked uncomfortable; the choir sounded mechanical. Peter stopped them.

"Are you at home in this position?" he asked Andrew. "What do you see as the main task here?

Andrew thought for a moment. "To try to get the music right?"

"Is this an equation to be worked through and checked, or is it to do with people?" asked Peter. "We are trying to get to the emotional heart of this music. Try holding your arms here." Peter adjusted the position of Andrew's arms. "Now relax your shoulders. When you start the music, breathe in. Try to copy the breathing of the singers. Watch how they hold their heads; watch their faces. See what they are feeling. Try to anticipate what they want. Encourage them. Don't worry about what you are doing so much; watch the singers."

Andrew tried again. The early bars of the music were stiff and forced, but Andrew could be seen to be concentrating on the singers. He began unconsciously to mimic their breathing, their posture and even their facial expressions. The sound warmed, and Andrew was visibly encouraged. His movements became more expressive, more thoughtful. The choir responded again.

"Now we are making this music together," said Peter. "The singers don't need you to work it out for them. What interests them is you. What do you want? But for them to know what you want, you have to stop telling them what to do."

Andrew tried the second piece; the Mendelssohn. He was clearly enjoying himself. The choir sang happily.

"Ok, this is good," Peter interrupted, "but now you have just let go. Now you are just having fun, That's ok! But the choir is wondering 'What does he want?' 'What should we do?' So now you need to think about how you would like this to sound. Now, it is cheerful; it's happy! That's nice – but is it what you want? Or is the music more passionate; more thoughtful? How do you feel about it?"

Andrew collected himself and tried again. He looked more concentrated. His hands moved together in front of him and his upper body swayed a little in support of their movements. The choir responded instantly with a surge of warmth and emotion. The piece ended, with Andrew looking a little shocked.

"The leadership you give is immediately visible," said Peter. "The choir see you and see what you want, and we hear the result immediately." Andrew nodded, still looking a little stunned by the experience, and made his way back to his seat, his colleagues smiling as he passed them.

Margaret was next to stand in front of the choir. She smiled confidently and gestured for them to begin. They sang strongly and powerfully. As the piece began to unfold, Margaret was clearly caught up with the beauty of the piece. Her gestures became more expansive, the choir became more ragged.

"OK," said Peter. "That was great. But you were carried away by the loveliness of the music!"

Margaret smiled bashfully in agreement.

"It is beautiful!" said Peter. "But we have to think about what we want and not just to bask in this beauty. You are a very warm person, and the choir is enjoying singing with you, but you are not really leading them anywhere. They don't yet have a vision. May I?"

Peter stepped behind Margaret and took both of her wrists in his. He moved her arms lower, and made a gesture for the choir to begin. Her movements, now controlled by Peter, were more precise and more impactful. The choir sang richly. Peter let go of her arms and Margaret restarted the choir. Her gestures were different, more like the ones that Peter had helped her to create; she still looked radiant, but more thoughtful. The choir sang warmly; there was more shape to the music. Margaret called for a swell in volume and the choir responded. She successfully called for a quieter passage, and the choir dropped their volume. As the piece drew to an end, Margaret gestured more expansively and the singers reached the end of the piece in full voice. Everyone, the singers included, applauded. Margaret put both of her hands to her face and laughed in disbelief.

"So now we have some vision!" said Peter. "Now you are taking people somewhere!"

Margaret conducted the second piece with great aplomb and returned to her seat, looking flushed, and her colleagues congratulated her warmly. John came to the front.

He lifted his head and smiled at the choir. Everything started well. John asked for a small *accelerando*, calling for a faster tempo, and the choir responded. A little later he tried to slow the tempo down again, but the choir had lost the beat. The singing ground to a halt in disarray. John looked crestfallen.

"Now I think you are like a driver with a new car," said Peter, kindly. "You are thinking: 'What can I do with this? Will it go faster? Will it stop suddenly?' That's ok. It's an amazing feeling, yes?" Peter looked at John. "Here is this group of wonderful singers, and they will do anything you tell them! But it doesn't really work like that. You have to be the glue that binds it all together. If you just take the choir for a spin like a Lamborghini, it's just a joyride. It's great fun, but it doesn't really go anywhere. It's just a stunt. So you need to think about where you want to go."

John looked chastened. He started again. He set a slightly slower pace and held to it, listening carefully to the choir. Something in his gestures encouraged them and he responded to that; the music became richer, more emotional, the voices seeming to blend together more evenly.

"Bravo!" said Peter. "Now we are not putting this wonderful machine through its paces, we are appreciating its beauty. We are exploring what we can do together. Let's try the next piece – and I want to try something a little difficult, a little dangerous. I want you, John, to think more about the individual singers. I want you to focus on each of their individual voices as well as on the overall sound. And maybe you will want to call for something a little extra or a little different from any one of them. And singers, if you begin to feel inspired, I want you to stand up. You don't have to stand up, but if it is going well and you feel inspired, just get up on your feet."

John started the second piece. It progressed well, the singers singing with conviction and precision. John tried to focus on their individual voices, occasionally making a slight gesture or smiling at one singer in particular. The tenor stood to his feet. John was visibly encouraged. His gestures became less urging; less demanding. In the early stages he could be seen to be willing the choir to be inspired, to be pouring in motivational encouragement. Now he was beginning to enjoy the sound that the choir was producing. The soprano got to her feet, her voice suddenly opening up thrillingly, more than before, on the highest notes. The alto and bass quickly joined her, and the choir finished the piece with great gusto, leaving the last notes of the piece reverberating through the church.

John looked thrilled. "Excellent," said Peter. "Remember the subtle difference between motivation and inspiration. You can try as hard as you like, but you can't force people to be inspired. Inspiration comes from inside them; it's between you and them. They have to feel the potential reward. They have to think, 'Yes! This feels better. I am getting something new from this. This is what I want.'"

He smiled at John: "Well done."

It was Roger's turn. He came nervously to the conductor's spot, his height and bulk making even Peter look less tall. They started with a chorale, from JS Bach's *St Matthew's Passion*. The tune is relatively simple, and is adapted from a 17th century hymn tune that was itself adapted from an early secular love song. It sounds like a love song; simple, thrilling and passionate. It is not necessary to be a Christian, or even a believer, to recognize the emotion of the tune; in Bach's setting, it becomes a deeply moving piece that seems to convey both great grief and some possibility of consolation, even hope. In the early verses of the chorale, the mood is sombre; as it progresses, hope seems to emerge with growing conviction.

Roger began to conduct. He established a good tempo, beating time with his right hand in the conventional way, signalling clearly, as each new line began, trying to call on an individual singer when a particular contribution was needed. It was not a bad effort.

After a couple of stanzas, Peter stopped him.

"You are used to giving clear instructions. You feel the need to tell people what to do," said Peter. "Have you ever been to Rome?" he asked unexpectedly.

"Um, yes, I have," replied Roger.

"Then you may have seen the traffic policemen at major road junctions," said Peter, smiling. "You know how Italian drivers are. There don't seem to be any rules, or any road markings, and everyone just drives onto the junction and tries to get to the other side. So the traffic policemen have to take charge, to stop people from killing one another. They make bold, visible gestures." Peter imitated a Roman traffic policeman, holding up a hand dramatically to forbid the imaginary traffic from coming on, waving vigorously to call another lane of traffic forward. Everyone laughed quietly.

"Only with you it is more as if you are marshalling tanks on Salisbury Plain," said Peter. "You have a military background maybe?"

Roger stared at Peter as if he was a fortune teller who had revealed some remarkable secret about his life.

"It's not that difficult really," smiled Peter. "Army training leaves its mark, you know?"

Roger smiled. "Not the army, the navy," he corrected Peter. "I was a Royal Marine volunteer."

"But you seem to grasp the music also," said Peter.

"Well, I used to sing in a church choir. We used to sing this at Easter time," Roger agreed. "I always loved singing it. It's very beautiful."

"It is beautiful" agreed Peter. "So let's work on these arm movements. Don't worry about the beat. You have the right pulse, that's excellent. Keep to that. May I?"

He stood behind Roger and took both of his wrists in his own. Despite Peter's own height, it looked comical, like a puppet master controlling an oversize puppet.

Conducting through Roger's arms and hands, Peter started the choir again and took them through a verse of the chorale. Roger's gestures, controlled by Peter, stayed around Roger's waist level and were expressive but constrained. When Peter wanted the music to swell slightly, he amplified his gestures, but not dramatically. The verse ended with its haunting, peaceful fall.

"Ok?"

Roger nodded and took a deep breath. He looked at the choir, smiled slightly and brought them in. The first verse sounded lovely. Roger began the second verse. His eyes closed and his shoulders relaxed. His gestures were more like those that Peter had showed him, but something else was clearly happening. Tears appeared on Roger's face; as the song continued, they began to stream unheeded down his face and into his beard. He looked transported; conducting calmly and expressively, his eyes still closed, tears coursing down his face. Unseen by Roger, and unbidden, the choir came to their feet one after the other, in quick succession. Peter, also unseen by Roger, gestured for the choir to continue singing further verses. The music filled the church, soaring and dying away with each verse; heartrending yet redemptive. Roger seemed to know when the last verse had been reached. He opened his eyes and blinked, surprised to find the choir all standing and his colleagues staring at him intently, their eyes shining.

"Excuse me," said Roger, taking a handkerchief from his pocket and drying his tear-stained face.

Peter glanced at Roger and judged that he was emotionally intact.

"You are a great conductor!" Peter said, simply. "What happened?"

"Well, I remember the music," said Roger quietly. "And when I was singing in the church choir, it was easy. I had a good treble voice and I just opened my mouth and this lovely sound came out. I didn't have to think about it. And we would sing hymns, psalms and everyday stuff and that was nice. I like hymns. But then, sometimes, you'd sing an anthem or something – like this piece – and it would be wonderful. You would hear your own voice contributing to this beautiful sound, and that was exhilarating; it inspired you to sing better and then everyone would get better and it was just..."

Roger's voice trailed off and he dabbed his eyes again with his handkerchief.

"So, I was taken back to those days. It was like being 11 years old again and this lovely sound just pouring out of my mouth, when I suddenly realized that this was what the singers would be experiencing. Except that they are better than I was."

Roger smiled at the choir, who smiled back warmly.

"And I just realized what they needed from me. They needed me to deliver the music to them. I just had to let the music sort of flow through me to them, and maybe help it a little bit, if I could..."

Roger stumbled to a halt.

"You have the makings of a great conductor," said Peter, warmly, putting his hand on Roger's shoulder. "You offer the music to the singers. Do you want to try the next piece?"

"I think I'm all washed up," said Roger, bashfully. Peter looked at him carefully.

"Then I think we'll call it a day. Thank you all. Can you all show your appreciation for one another?"

The team and choir applauded each other warmly. Roger re-joined the team. His colleagues patted his arm or his back as he passed them; John stood up and put his arm briefly around Roger's shoulder. Margaret gave him a kiss on the cheek. "That was marvelous," she said, smiling brightly. "Thank you," said Roger, quietly.

* * *

On the journey back, everyone seemed to be lost in a reverie. They all looked happy, and thoughtful.

Back at the business school, they assembled for a final time in the smaller conference room, with the whiteboard still covered in the ideas that they had noted from the previous sessions. Everyone seemed comfortable in each other's presence. Some of the emotion of the morning's session with the singers still lingered.

"OK," said Mark. "Let's do a little washing up. We have a list of ideas from yesterday," he gestured at the whiteboard. "Pretty much every idea or concept we feel we had taken out of the sessions to date. Now let's have a go at adding some lessons from this morning – but don't worry if you find it hard to put those into words!"

The team all smiled quietly in agreement.

"Remember what I said about needing to experience things if we want to really change how we think and how we behave?" Mark asked.

The team nodded.

"Well, we all experienced things in that session today, and with Gunnar and Marika yesterday and with the jazz players and with Piers, and some of them were very thought-provoking and some were more emotional. Emotion is something that performing artists are entirely familiar with and work with, but it's entirely uncommon in business. I would like to suggest that you have probably learned something quite profound about leadership today, but that you may not only struggle to put that into words, but might not want to, or be able to. That's fine. Because the lesson is in here." Mark tapped his stomach lightly with his fist.

The team shuffled a little on their seats, but looked relaxed; smiling.

"Right, let's go for it!" said Mark. "Let's have your reflections on today's session – your thoughts about 'visible leaders listening to people.'"

The team all laughed a little.

"And let's not labour too much on that. I suspect that those lessons are all locked away." He tapped his chest. "Let's sum up what we feel we've learned and begin to apply that to your own situation that we discussed yesterday, and see if we can draw up some kind of action plan."

The team sat up in their chairs, as if collecting their thoughts, and the final session of the programme began.

A Great
Performance

"Well, gentlemen, Margaret. How was the programme?" Jack Isherwood asked the board.

The team had returned from the business school the previous evening and were meeting in the boardroom for a 'council of war' with the CEO first thing the following morning. The constant traffic on the bypass created its familiar background hum. The occasional passenger jet roared on take-off from nearby London Luton airport.

"Um, eye-opening, I think is the word, Jack," said John.

There was a general murmur of agreement from his colleagues.

"For me, it was emotional", said Roger, smiling rather bashfully.

"Emotional?" asked Isherwood, quizzically.

"Roger discovered his inner conductor," said Margaret.

"You'll have to tell me later, Roger!" said Isherwood, managing a smile. "Anything else? What were the main takeaways? Anything that may help us with the re-pitch?"

The team looked around at one another, a little helplessly.

"Ok, I'll go first," said John. "We need to create some new ensembles to tackle the problem. And we need to take hierarchy and status out of those ensembles."

"We need to involve people from across the whole organization," said Andrew. "We have too many Hamlets and not enough gravediggers."

Isherwood looked a little puzzled, but gestured for the team to continue.

"I could maybe show you if we had a choir in here, Jack," said Roger, "but I'm not sure if I can describe it. It's something like: 'We need to open ourselves up to our teams; we need to be more transparent to them and encourage them to express themselves."

Roger looked embarrassed but Margaret came to his rescue.

"That's very well put, Roger. That's exactly what we need to do. We need to forge a real connection with people and build a greater level of trust."

"We need to let people improvise," said Rory. "And encourage them to surprise us; we need to help them to be brilliant."

"We need to find the art in what we do," said John. "That was the big one for me. We need to be technically brilliant, which we hopefully are, but we need to put on a better performance, in the widest sense."

"Yes," agreed Andrew. "We need to get some artistry into what we do to help us beat the competition."

"We need to find our theatre of operation, the beating heart of the organization," said Margaret. "We talked about this in our final brainstorm session with Mark, our facilitator, and realized that the heart of the organization isn't the factory, or the people who interface with our clients – too many Hamlets again!" She smiled around at her colleagues, who nodded knowingly. "We think our theatre of operation is the interface between everyone in our organization and everyone in the client's operation. It's about our engineers and their engineers as much as it is about Roger's team and the client management. So we need to get more people at that interface, and our main job should be to support them."

"We need to trust one another more; trust everybody more," said Rory. "We need to play to each other's strengths and put our faith in them. Maybe we need to sacrifice control in return for inspiration."

"And we need to think about the inputs that are creating our outputs," said Roger. "We need to think about what people are really doing to create what we see later as spreadsheets; as numbers. It's the inputs that really matter."

"Ok, ok, enough!" said Isherwood, throwing up his hands in mock horror. "You've clearly come away with a lot of stuff to think about. I look forward to talking to you about it. But I need to remind you that we face the worst crisis in the company's history. It's nice to see you looking so fired up, but we need to knuckle down and address the problem. Nothing else matters at the moment except this re-pitch. We have to focus on nothing else for the next few weeks. Our survival depends on it."

"Jack, if I may," said John. "If we seem inappropriately cheerful, it's because we *are* all quite fired up. We covered a lot of ground at the end of yesterday in our final session together, and we have the bones of a plan of action. And it must only be the bones of a plan at the moment, because we're going to ask other people to put the flesh on those bones."

"But the main thing is," John continued before Isherwood could make a comment, "we are going to put together the best pitch our client has ever seen, and we are going to win that account back. And if we don't win it back – though we will!" Isherwood smiled. "If we can't keep the account, then we are going to create something new and wonderful from whatever we have left as a business. None of us is kidding ourselves about how painful that will be, and it's not the outcome anyone wants, but, whatever happens, Jack, this will not be the end. We'll just have to be more creative. But first, in fact, we *are* going to win back the contract."

Isherwood said nothing for some moments and looked thoughtfully at his colleagues.

"Gentlemen. Margaret," he said finally. "I don't need to tell you again how serious the situation is, but I like what I'm hearing. Tell me about this plan. Or the bones of this plan."

"First," said John, "we need to let everyone in the business know where we stand. I know that is going to be unsettling, but we need help from people at every level of the company, and we can't let some people in on the problem and not others. We have to be open. I think if we are honest about everything, they will understand and be supportive."

"Are you sure about telling everyone, John?" asked Isherwood. "I mean, it could cause a lot of anxiety. We don't need everyone cracking up on us right now."

"Our people are loyal and tough, Jack" said Margaret, "and you've always been straight with them. That's why they are loyal. So although this is scary news, it's better they hear it straight from you, now, so that they can all get behind the pitch."

"Ok," said Isherwood. "I'll ask Janet to set up a session with all staff members in the next few days, and I'll fly up to have the same session with the Glasgow plant in the afternoon, so no one finds out through the rumour mill."

"Do you mind if we all play a part in that, Jack? Just to say a few words each. We want everyone to see that we're all involved in this. And I suggest that I talk to the union representatives the day before so they don't feel that we've sprung something on them."

"Ok," said Isherwood. "Then what?"

"The five of us would like to steer this through together, if you're happy with that," said John. "We're going to meet informally on a daily basis to make sure we're all on track. And we're each going to embed ourselves in a number of task forces. We need to pull together teams of people from across the company; not just managers and certainly not just directors. People from the shop floor. These teams can explore every aspect of our business on the client account – the products, the engineering, our working practices, our relationship with the client. We're going to be absolutely open with everyone and make those task forces into real ensembles. We're going to ask them what we can do to make our client happier; to improve our relationship."

"And then we're going to take everyone's ideas, and turn that into the best presentation the client has ever seen," said Roger. "We're going to throw out all of the numbers – they've got those anyway – and we're going to show the client how bloody wonderful we are and why they'd be crazy to let us go. We are going to put on a performance like they've never seen before!"

"And Jack, if you will sign off the cost," said Margaret, "I'd like to get a video team in to do some filming. We want to show the client the real people behind our operation."

"That sounds like a plan," said Isherwood. "In fact, it sounds like the best plan I've heard in a long time. It looks as if that programme was exactly what we needed at exactly the right time. Well…" Isherwood paused. "Maybe six months earlier would have been even better! However. Well done, all of you!" he concluded briskly. "Let's get started. I'd be grateful if I could join your daily meetings from time to time so that I am up to speed, and let me know if there's anything specific I can do to help at any stage. We should get confirmation of the date for the presentation later today, and it will be sometime around the 10th of next month. So we've got three weeks to crack this. Good luck."

＊＊＊

It was the day of the re-pitch to the client.

Jack Isherwood and the five board members were sitting around a large conference table, along with two colleagues from the Luton plant and one from Glasgow. Michael Browning, the client purchasing director, was there with four of his colleagues – the same team which had seen the first presentation by Roger and his team.

Isherwood got to his feet.

"Ladies and gentlemen, thank you for coming, and thank you in particular for giving us this second chance to present; I know it is exceptional."

"Not at all, Jack," said Browning. "Our companies go back a long way. It's the least we could do."

"Well, thank you all the same," said Isherwood. "First, let me apologize for our side being a little mob-handed. We wanted to do this a bit differently. We wanted you to meet all the board members – these are the people who steer our company and I know that you don't always get to meet them. And then we particularly wanted you to meet some of the other people you never get to meet – some of our engineering and production team.

"One of the things that we want to say to you today is that, if we can continue to work together – and we very much hope we can – we believe that one of the things that will help us to work better together is a greater degree of contact between more, different, members of our team and their counterparts in your organization. I'd like to explain what we mean by that in a moment. First of all, I want to say that in the past few weeks we have gone back to the grassroots of our own organization and asked people for their ideas about ways in which we could work differently with your team to produce exceptional results. I have to say that I was humbled by the level of energy and creativity that we found in our people, and I want to say now that I felt ashamed that we have not done that enough in the past.

"This is a day for confessions, ladies and gentlemen and, if you will allow us, we are going to bare our souls to you a little. We would like you to see us as we really are, and then decide if we are the people you would like to keep working with. We sincerely hope that you will decide we are, but if you do not, we will have the satisfaction of knowing that we have shared everything with you to help you make your decision."

Isherwood cleared his throat.

"My own piece of soul-baring is to tell you just how much we want to keep your business. I won't dissemble with you. If we lose your business we will regroup and carry on, but I don't mind telling you I would see that as a personal failure. For nearly all the time I have worked for this company, we have had your business. The two go together in my mind. I find it unthinkable that we should not have your business and I feel a great sense of responsibility for the fact that we have, it seems, become complacent. We know that we are doing a good job for you, but it was a massive shock to hear Michael say…" – Isherwood looked towards Browning – "that you had seen more exciting presentations from other companies. That it seemed that those companies would be more exciting to work with. We have clearly failed to stay ahead of the game.

"We are going to try to do whatever it takes to show you how much we care about your business, and that we are not complacent; that we are still capable of new thinking. We have some particular new ideas that we would like to run past you today, but also some suggestions that we believe will build constant improvement and constant innovation into our relationship. We have explored our organization from top to bottom in the past few weeks, and it has been an invigorating experience. We hope that we can share some of that excitement with you today. And now I would like to hand you over to Roger, who will chair our presentation today."

"Good morning everyone," said Roger. "It's a pleasure to see you, as always. I have some very good news for you. I am not going to say much today."

The client team laughed politely.

"I have realized recently – we have all realized – that there has been too much of me and my team in our relationship and not enough of our wider organization. And I'd like to start to correct that by introducing people that you don't normally meet, and they would like to talk about some of their ideas. You may or may not want to proceed with all of them, but we think that it demonstrates the kind of thinking that, together..." – Roger spread out his arms to encompass everyone in the room – "we must be capable of. I'd like to hand you over to Malcolm Irvine, from our Scottish plant." Roger put up an image of a component for a transmission system. "Malcolm works in the unit that produce this little beauty for you, and he has an interesting idea."

The engineer got to his feet. "Ladies and gentlemen, good morning," he said in a strong Glaswegian accent. "Forgive me, I don't do a lot of presenting. And forgive me also if you have difficulty in understanding my accent, but we do have a translator here..." – he indicated Rory Campbell. "Rory understands Glaswegian quite well, even though he comes from the wrong part of Scotland himself."

Everyone smiled.

"We've been making this part for you for a long time," he continued. "It's a great little part, and it has a remarkably good return rate, which is excellent. We still make this to the original specification. It's never changed in all the time that I've been working at the plant. And it struck me recently that the rate of returns has actually been going down in recent years, even though the specification hasn't changed. And that said to me, that maybe you have begun to use these parts in a lower spec vehicle, and *that* is why the level of returns is getting better. I'm wondering if we are over-engineering this part for some of your requirements, and that some of them are now being used in vehicles that are not producing the same level of torque and so don't require the same level of engineering. If I'm right, we could save you money by producing a new part in the appropriate numbers to a slightly lower spec."

He sat down. A few of the client team glanced at each other.

"Thank you, Malcolm," said Roger. "Now, if I may, I'd like to introduce John Watson, who is from our Luton plant. John's team produces these components for you." Roger put up a slide of two components for an air conditioning unit.

"Thank you. My name is John Watson. This is a very simple idea really. We supply these parts for you and you assemble them when you put the air conditioning units together. But I was looking at a unit the other day and I realized that you don't really need to have two separate parts. I've rigged up a little prototype, if I can just show you." He took something out of a plastic bag by his feet. "Here's one I made earlier!" he joked, revealing a prototype of the new part. "This does exactly the same job as the two components, and has the same fittings, but it is cheaper for us to manufacture it as one component, and it should save you time in the assembly process. Um. Thank you." John smiled bashfully and sat down.

One of the client team raised her eyebrows, pursed her lips and nodded almost imperceptibly.

"We've got one more engineering idea for you," said Roger, "and I'd like to pass you back to Jack for this one, because it involves an investment decision."

"Thank you, Roger," said Isherwood. "We've been researching the market for machinery for the major components that we produce for you, and a Japanese company is offering some completely new tooling that would mean we could produce these components faster, cheaper and at a remarkably high level of precision. This would mean better, cheaper parts for you. The investment for us is substantial…" – Isherwood mentioned a multi-million-pound sum – "but we would be delighted to make this investment if we can indeed retain your business and hopefully negotiate a longer contract for production of these units to give us the opportunity to recoup our costs. Obviously this one needs some more discussion, but we would like just to add it to the mix at this point."

"Thank you, Jack" said Roger. "Now on the manufacturing side, we have another development, and I'd like to ask Margaret Simons, our HR director, to talk to us about this. Margaret?"

"Thank you," said Margaret. "This is very straightforward, but it's very significant for us. We recently shared with all of our people the possibility that we would not retain your account. That would have repercussions for the two factories, obviously, and we like to be as upfront with our people as we can. More importantly, we've been working with task forces across the whole organization looking for good ideas, and – as Jack was saying – it's been quite wonderful how engaged everyone has been in the whole process. I mean whatever happens, if I'm allowed to say this," Margaret glanced a little nervously at Isherwood, "this has been a very positive process. It has brought everyone together." Isherwood nodded in agreement.

"We currently have two eight-hour shifts, eight in the morning till four in the afternoon, and four till midnight," said Margaret. "Both plants have volunteered to add an extra four-hour shift from midnight till four in the morning, at double time. The proposal has the full backing of the unions, who have been very proactive. We've looked at the implications and have actually done some real-time rehearsal of the whole process – at four in the morning, with everyone involved!"

The client team smiled.

"And we now know for certain that we can run our servicing and maintenance schedule in the four hours between four and eight. The new shift would potentially increase our production capacity by one third, which has major implications on what we can deliver for you on many fronts. It would also create new job opportunities at both plants, which is very pleasing. It's potentially a very exciting development."

The client team exchanged more glances.

"Thank you, Margaret," said Roger. "Now, I'd like to introduce our backroom boy, Andrew Gibbon, our finance director. I don't think any of you have met him before. I'm afraid that Andrew doesn't get out much!"

"I'm afraid that's true," said Andrew, "but I hope to get out more in the future. It's a great pleasure to be here today and to meet you all." Andrew smiled at the client team. "I've also been a part of one of the task forces that we've been running for the past several weeks, and it's been great to stick my head in the boiler room, as it were. We get a bit fixated with spreadsheets in our department, and it's nice to be reminded that the numbers represent real things! The inputs that go into creating the outputs." He glanced at his colleagues, smiling a little nervously.

"We've had an idea about our financial relationship," he continued. "I noticed how committed our people are to delivering on schedule, and to sticking to our quality control agreements. I gather that our record with you is very strong on both fronts."

"That's entirely true," Browning agreed.

"Well, with Jack's agreement," said Andrew, "we've decided that we'd like to offer to put our money where our mouth is. We'd like to propose a new billing arrangement where we agree a base price for every item that we supply, and then a bonus for each line that is entirely dependent on our hitting agreements for on-time delivery and quality control. We're confident that we will continue to hit our targets, but this would give you the added security of knowing that if we fail to meet targets, we are penalized financially."

"Thank you Andrew," said Roger. "Now, if we may, we have a short film to show you. Margaret arranged for a video team to follow us around, and we'd like to show you the result. The point of this is that we realized that the relationship between our two companies isn't about my relationship with Martin here," Roger gestured towards one of the client managers, "or with how our account teams get on, or even all of us with all of you." He smiled around the room. "The relationship that really matters is between all of our colleagues and all of the people on your side who work with our products. Every single one of them has some input into what we produce for you, and they all do their work with pride and passion.

They are very proud to be producing components that go into your wonderful cars. You hear them say it to their friends: 'We make the so-and-so unit for that model,' when they see the car on the streets.

"I mean, that has really been brought home to me in the past few weeks. I haven't been spending enough time on the factory floor or with the design teams. That's where a big part of our beating heart is. But that beating heart…" Roger frowned and looked a bit uncomfortable. "I'm in danger of getting a bit poetic here – that beating heart only works if it's beating in tandem with your operation. What we do has to mesh completely with what you do. We have to have a real connection. So the real beating heart of our operation is what we do together. It's all of our guys and all of your guys. Am I making any sense?" he said, looking around the room.

"Yes you are, Roger," said Browning.

"Well, anyway, this film will show you the people who do the work that produces the stuff that your guys require. And we wanted to make them into a bit of, you know, the heroes and heroines, because they are what drives the whole thing; they are who we are."

Roger broke off, looking a bit embarrassed, and started the video. The professionally produced film cut rapidly between scenes of meetings taking place; of people drawing diagrams on whiteboards; of engineers looking at 3D images on computer screens. It showed the production line and individual workers carrying out their tasks. It showed the maintenance team working in the middle of the night and the cleaners arriving in the early hours of the morning. It showed people eating in the canteen and the handover between shifts. The board members could be seen in conversation with groups of people, sometimes in meeting rooms, often on the factory floor. The video cut to aerial shots of the two plants, making both Glasgow and Luton seem surprisingly glamorous, zooming in on the entire workforce of both plants, standing in their respective car parks and waving up. It ended with a series of shots of individuals, with their names and job functions displayed in subtitles as they talked in their own words about their roles.

The client team watched intently.

"I just want to leave you with this image," said Roger, putting up a picture of a family driving one of the client's cars. "This is really the beating heart of all of our efforts: your customers, driving well-engineered, safe, efficient, exciting vehicles. This is what it really is all about. We have been very proud to play our part in this process for the past 15 years and, ladies and gentlemen," Roger looked at the client team, smiling, "we would very much love to continue to be a part of that process. Thank you."

Roger sat down and Jack Isherwood got to his feet again.

"Thank you, Roger. I'd just like to conclude with something we see as very important. We've all talked about the task forces that we have set up. The board went on a programme recently, and they worked with performing artists – dancers, actors, conductors and so on – trying to get into the mindset of these artists; how they go about creating a winning performance. And one of the things that I have really taken on board from what they have told me about this is the need to involve every member of the team for a successful operation. You know, that you can't put on a play if everyone is Hamlet: you need the gravediggers, and Rosencrantz and Guildenstern, and the soldiers and the players in the play within the play."

The client team looked a bit quizzical.

"Ah, bear with us on this!" said Isherwood, smiling. "It's become a bit of mantra for us. 'Get the right people in the room!' We hope that we have gone some way with this today by having John and Malcom with us here." Isherwood smiled at the two engineers. "And we are determined to involve our whole cast from now on, to work as a real ensemble. So we are going to keep the task forces going, and they are going to include people from cleaners all the way up to board members and we are going to focus on constant improvement and constant innovation.

"Now, on that topic, I would like to tell you that we have changed the role of Rory Campbell here…" Isherwood put his hand on Rory's shoulder as he sat beside him, "from chief technical officer to chief innovation officer. And I'd like Rory to tell us about a new idea that he has."

"Good morning all," said Rory, getting to his feet. "Well, as you've heard, we are going to install a number of permanent task forces to look at every aspect of our operation, and I will lead the technical group concerned with improvement and innovation. We're going to involve people from all levels, again. People from the production line as well as our technical designers. People like Malcolm Irvine and John Watson here…" – Rory gestured at the two engineers – "who had the interesting ideas we've seen here today. These guys don't have 'innovation' in their job title, but actually, they are the people who came up with two clever ideas that could make things better for all of us."

Rory smiled across at the engineers, who looked embarrassed but proud.

"But we need somebody else in the room," continued Rory. "We need your guys involved so they can tell us what you need and give us feedback. So we'd like to make one final proposal. We'd like to suggest that we set up a joint R&D unit, with key people from your operation and our operation working together at your factory for several days per week. We'd like these people to share ideas and issues and practices, then to come back to the next session with new ideas and recommendations. We see this as a key component of how we can work together as productively as possible, and we are confident that some important ideas will emerge from this. We're confident that this new unit could make further improvements; save time and money; create better products. If we keep going at this, we're convinced that we can be more creative together; that we could create a great performance together. Jack was saying just now," Rory glanced at Isherwood, "that we've got a bit obsessed with the whole idea of performance lately, and it's true. We feel that maybe we haven't been looking beyond the technical issues. We aim to be technically perfect, and we think that we do a good job. But maybe we haven't been so focused on the art of what we do, the overall performance; being not just excellent but amazing; being brilliant. Working together as a real partnership, making truly fantastic products. And that comes from the two of us, from how we interact together. We have to make a better connection with your team. And we think the joint innovation team would be a great start."

Rory sat down, looking a little flushed, and Isherwood got to his feet for the last time.

"Thank you again for this opportunity; we wanted to tell you more about why we think we can continue to give you what you need, and how we plan to raise our game. We've deliberately kept numbers out of this presentation. You saw those before and as you said, Michael," Isherwood smiled at Browning, "you know the numbers and they're not exciting in themselves! But if there is anything that we've said today that you need the numbers on, so that you can explore it more carefully, just let us know and Andrew here will provide the necessary. Thank you all again."

Browning stood up from his chair at the head of the table. "Thank you, all of you. I think I can speak for all my colleagues when I say that that was the most enjoyable presentation we have seen for a long while and the one that has given us most to think about. There's a lot of ideas in there and a lot of potential. A great performance!" He smiled at Rory, who smiled back. "Thank you again," said Browning, looking over at Isherwood, who returned his smile.

Isherwood's team stood up, thanked their opposite numbers and headed for the door.

"Let me show you out," said Browning. "Jack, I'll call you in the morning after I've talked to all my colleagues."

"Thank you, Michael," said Isherwood.

Ten Lessons from the Performing Arts

Jack Isherwood and his team kept their key account.

Isherwood took the call from Browning the following morning to hear that the client team had agreed unanimously to keep working with Isherwood's company. The idea of the joint R&D team housed at the client's main plant was warmly welcomed, as were the potential increases in production capacity brought about by the new night shifts and the investment in retooling at both plants. Andrew's new billing system, locking the company's remuneration into the delivery of time and quality commitments was seen as a clever innovation and a welcome commitment. Both the product innovations recommended in the presentation were taken up by the client. Over the following years, a steady stream of improvements and the occasional truly significant innovation flowed out of the increased collaboration between the two companies and the improved communication within Isherwood's company between employees at all levels. Negotiations began about length of contracts and production volumes that would recoup Isherwood's company's extra investments and overtime costs over the years to come.

The board remained committed to the concept of 'performance' and for the rest of their careers would be heard occasionally to say things to each other, to the bafflement of others. "Too many Hamlets," Margaret might say. "Haven't got the right people in the room," Andrew would agree. "We are looking and not seeing," John would venture; "we don't have the right connection yet." "This is great, but where is the art in it?" Rory would ask his engineers; "it's good, but it's not beautiful. We're not going to win with this. We need to make it amazing." "I need to be in charge but not in control," Roger would remind himself. "I need to offer the music to the players."

* * *

Although Isherwood's company and his board members are fictionalized, they are based on real companies, real people, real problems and the real experiences of senior executives on arts-based development programmes designed and led by Dr Mark Powell, co-author of this book, over a period of many years.

Delegates' experiences on these programmes lead to realizations and understandings that are always significant and sometimes profound. These new understandings can change how people see the world around them, how they engage with their friends and colleagues and even with their partners and their families, but it is impossible to predict exactly which aspect of any particular programme will hit home with any individual delegate.

Sometimes, it is a session with a poet or a painter that suddenly makes an emotional impact. Sometimes it is a challenging theatre-based exercise, or the experience of watching professional dancers working wonderfully together, or the surprisingly profound experience of conducting a choir of trained singers and being able to change, dramatically, the sound that they make, simply by means of gesture and the way in which one holds one's body.

Because one can never tell which 'message' or idea will be taken up by any individual, it is impossible to offer a definitive list of the take-outs that a close encounter with the performing arts may offer. In the authors' experience, however, the list of ten fundamental lessons set out below covers most of the bases. These have been set out as a list of questions that you might like to ask yourself. The lessons may well be applicable to you as a person as much as they are to your working life: they are about attitudes, mindsets and ways of being in the world. They all stem from simple yet profound realizations about how we behave in relation to other people, and they have a dramatic impact on all of our behaviours, both private and professional.

Performing artists experience the world differently from the way in which the rest of us experience it. There is nothing magical about this, they just have different perspectives and priorities, all of which flow from their overriding obsession with putting on a great performance. As a performing artist, there is no place to hide. If one is 'having a bad day', it is plain for all to see. It is impossible to hide behind fellow performers, because the defects in one's own performance affect the performance of others. It is impossible to be a 'disengaged' performer: the performing artist is their own performance and their personal energy flows directly into their performance.

Businesses – organizations, places of work, call them what you will – tend to behave very differently from groups of performing artists.

In our previous book, *My Steam Engine is Broken: Taking the organization from the industrial era to the age of ideas*[3], we argued that the managerial mindset of many organizations has remained stuck in the industrial era. Organizations, in general, are still obsessed with control, measurement and efficiency, in a way that was deemed appropriate in the days of scientific management and the 'one right way' of doing things, but is entirely inappropriate in a knowledge economy. Organizations are terrified of getting things wrong and, as a result, are becoming incapable of getting things right. The human energy of the members of the organization is channelled and stifled; the potentially joyful exuberance of co-creation is deliberately suppressed. The creative potential innate in any combination of people and ideas is destroyed by the insistence that there must be no surprises; that the best outcome is already known and desired.

But the world of business is becoming increasingly aware of the heavy financial cost of wasted human energy. Successive surveys reveal that alarming numbers of people are effectively 'disengaged' from their employers, to a greater or lesser extent. They turn up for work and go through the motions, but their heart is not in it. Their employers have failed to make them feel they are an important and significant part of the endeavour. This is, quite literally, unimaginable in the performing arts. Performing artists are all volunteers; they are all passionately 'engaged' in their performance; they have signed up for the overall project and they are dedicated to its success.

Performing artists are also highly disciplined. They get together to put on a show – the best show they are capable of producing – with remarkably few resources, and they will deliver that show, without fail, on schedule. Rehearsals will start at such and such a time and so many weeks later the show will go live, at a precise hour on a precise day, in front of a paying audience. Most businesses fail to deliver even minor projects on time and within budget, even without the additional challenge of producing something new, exciting and novel in the same timeframe. The difference is, of course, that the performing artists are committed to the project and equal before the task, and so will do whatever it takes, willingly and joyfully, to get the show on the road.

In their personal lives, people are increasingly becoming more and more 'engaged' – involving themselves in a variety of different communities; taking on unpaid roles with great enthusiasm and commitment. The world of business has the opportunity to tap into this great reservoir of human energy and engagement, but it will need to change its mindset in order to be able to do so. Organizations need to make the fundamental shift away from seeing employees as resources to be managed and towards seeing them as fellow artists in the same performance – because these fellow performers will then feel very differently about their own roles.

This is not a simple thing to do; once we have adopted a particular mindset, we tend to analyze every problem in terms of that mindset and to look for the kinds of solution with which we are familiar. One of the core arguments and takeaways of this book is that it is very difficult to change a mindset by means of traditional, logic-based learning experiences: a change in mindset tends to come about as a result of something experienced; something that takes one out of one's familiar territory and produces an 'aha!' moment that is experienced at a gut level. We have argued that exposing the world of business to the world of performing artists in an intimate, active way is one route to producing new, felt knowledge about how performing artists work together –

a way of working together that is radically different from the ways in which people within most organizations work together, yet which is highly functional and effective and which has innovation, creativity and a concentrated focus on the impact on the audience – the consumer – built into everything that it does.

The following list explores ten things that performing artists do, in order to deliver great, winning performances. At the heart of all of these things is one core realization: all great performers know that their own performance is utterly reliant on the performance of their fellow artists, and that they are as responsible for the performance of their fellows as they are for their own performance. An essential aspect of performing brilliantly is to do whatever one can to help one's fellow artists perform brilliantly; to be intensely focused on their behaviour and to give them whatever they need, second by second, to help them to be wonderful. This applies without regard to the importance of one's role in the performance; the same energy, focus and mutual assistance is needed from everyone, whether they have a starring role or a walk-on part. The quality of their performance then feeds back into one's own performance and the brilliance of the entire ensemble creates a marvelous experience for the audience: a truly great performance.

The commitment to enabling great individual contributions by fellow artists to ensure the overall success of the performance is at the heart of the performing arts. This is the exact opposite of the 'disengagement' experienced by employees in so many organizations.

If people began to see their work as a performance, as an exciting show that must be put on, daily, with the full commitment of the entire cast, the release of creative energy would be remarkable. If we, in our personal lives, as friends, partners, parents and community members, offered our fellow human beings the same kind of focus, trust and support that performing artists offer to their fellow artists, our lives would be greatly enriched.

Ten Lessons from the Performing Arts
1. What play are we in, and what is our role?

This sounds simple, but it is surprising how often we get this wrong.

In our fictional story, the real actor and business consultant, Piers Ibbotson, made a subtle point about his role as 'father at the school gates', in the show starring his daughter, called *My Life At School*. That particular role in the show is indeed very important, but it is a supporting, rather than leading, role. Our children need us to enable them to deliver a great performance, not to leave them standing in the shadow of our own brilliant performances. In modern life, we find ourselves playing many roles in many different shows. Our role within the main shows also changes, like that of an actor in a daily soap opera. Sometimes we have a leading role in the main story for the day; sometimes we have a walk-on part in a different storyline. Making the subtle changes needed to play each role to perfection makes for a winning performance. At work, for example, you may well be a senior executive, but 'senior executive behaviour' is not always welcome or appropriate – especially when we are trying to take status out of the equation to do something creative together. Understanding our different roles in this way is, perhaps paradoxically, at the heart of what has come to be called 'authenticity'. The person who plays the same role at all times, regardless of circumstance or context, is seen, quite rightly, as inauthentic. Real life is more subtle; we change our personas significantly and successfully as we move from role to role.

Reminding ourselves what the show we are currently in is called is a surprisingly useful approach. Our fictional company thought it was in the business of supplying excellently engineered products to the client's specification, and forgot that it was also its job to excite and inspire; that people like surprises as well as certainty. So they may have thought that their show was called, 'Supplying High Quality Parts To The Client's Specification', when perhaps the show was really called, 'Exploring Every Avenue To Help Our Client

Make Great Cars!' Their most important client was beginning to tire of the first show, and was tempted by other companies offering various versions of the second show; fortunately, they were able to rise to the occasion and put on a new and better show.

2. Where is our theatre of action?

The focal point of several kinds of operation is described as a 'theatre': the place where the crucial action happens – the stage, the operating theatre, the theatre of war, for example. In all of these theatres, there is a clear recognition that the most important people are those closest to the action: the actors; technicians; stage-hands; surgeons; anaesthetists; nurses; soldiers; tank drivers. Seniority, in the traditional sense, tends to increase as we move away from the actual theatre. The job of senior executives at the head of theatrical companies and hospitals and armies is to frame the overall strategy and to keep the organization running smoothly, but these people will – or should – be acutely aware that it is what happens in the theatre that is of defining importance.

This is a useful frame of mind. Where – in both our personal and our professional lives, is our theatre of action? Where is the beating heart of what we do?

The key to finding the right answer is to focus on the essential outcome, the bit that really matters. A well-disciplined and perfectly supplied army that cannot win battles in the theatre of war is not a good army. A brilliantly run theatre group that cannot put on an audience-pleasing show is not a successful theatre group.

Once it is obvious where our real theatre of action is located, it becomes clear who the key people are – the stars of the show – and how the operation should be organized. This is not a question of status, or even necessarily of reward. The infantryman is not 'more important' than the general, but he or she is vital to a successful outcome. Once we have decided where the beating heart of our operation is, it becomes clear who is vital to a successful outcome and who, no matter how senior, is essentially in a supporting role. Amongst those who are vital to a successful outcome, what matters most is their *esprit de corps*. If the rest of the organization has managed to make the people at the cutting edge of the operation dispirited and disheartened, things will go badly wrong very quickly.

In the modern business world, locating the theatre of operation can be difficult; the picture can be quite complex. An R&D department is clearly a beating heart, where talented people have starring roles in helping to design the future; manufacturing is another beating heart – we can't sell advanced products unless they are both well-made and aesthetically pleasing. Yet neither of these is the real theatre of action: the real theatre of action is always an interface; a place where the show is presented to an audience. In the case of our fictional company, the exact arena in which the show was presented to the audience was hard to define. The company's sales team had an interface with the client team, but the stage was, in reality, larger than this – the company's products were 'consumed' and experienced by large numbers of the client's engineers and ultimately by the client's car-buying customers. The real beating heart of our fictional company was where their engineers interfaced with the client's engineers, and these people were the stars of that show.

In our own personal and professional lives, there may also be several 'beating hearts', several key areas of vital importance, but in every case, there will be one key theatre of action: the place where what really matters happens; where our performance meets our audience, who then decide whether we have delivered a winning performance or not.

3. Have we built a trusting, connected partnership?

Any performance involving more than one player depends utterly on the relationship between the players. Performers must focus on their fellow players and connect, responding in the moment to a subtle reading of their intentions.

This mode of being is well described as 'looking and seeing'. It is very easy to look at someone and not really to see them, looking and seeing demands effort, but it leads to highly functional and deeply rewarding relationships, both in our personal and our professional lives.

Most of the communication that passes between people is non-verbal. Because we have language, we imagine the words we say have the greatest impact on the people around us. Words matter, obviously, when we want to exchange complex ideas and concepts. But understanding what someone wants, how they are feeling and what they are thinking of doing next does not require words. In both our private and our professional lives we forget, sometimes to our cost, that our intentions are written on our bodies and faces for all to see. Performing artists understand this and use it to form remarkable bonds, which allow them to anticipate and react to fellow performers in apparently magical ways. There is nothing magical about it; it comes from making the effort to focus on others and to sense what they are feeling and thinking. We are all born with this ability; we tend not to use it. We tend not to look and see and, as a result, we fail to make real connections with the people around us.

Something else that a good connection creates is complete trust – at least in the context of the performance. This works in our everyday lives too. It is not necessary to trust someone to act in a favourable way in every conceivable situation; it is entirely possible to trust someone completely within the limitations of a scenario where you share a common goal. Organizations seem to have lost sight of the essential role of trust within communities, or perhaps have forgotten that the organization is itself a community. The trust that comes from a good connection with others is the result of shared experiences; working openly and intimately to create a desired result. This kind of openness – which is emotionally challenging at first – is absent from most working scenarios.

Throwing people together and declaring that they are now 'a team' is nonsense. Given time, effort and openness to one another in the context of the shared task, however, a trusting, highly functional ensemble can soon be built. We can tell when it is beginning to work; there comes a time when we 'know' what the other person is thinking, and when they are or are not happy with something, and we know, instinctively and surprisingly, that they will be there for us; that we can trust them. When that happens, everything speeds up and many things become possible. If we don't have that connection and that trust, life is difficult. The creation of genuine teams has real and often dramatic benefits. The business organization that functions as a real ensemble is a formidable force.

It is essential to remember that status and hierarchy must be put to one side in a real ensemble. This is not to say there must be no leadership; people can and must be 'in charge', but not 'in control'. Status and hierarchy are real, unavoidable and in some ways even desirable, but in a genuine ensemble there must be equality before the task. Everyone has their role to play and no role is really more important than any other: every role has to be performed brilliantly to achieve the goal – a winning performance.

4. Are we rehearsing creatively?

Performing artists understand the fundamental importance of rehearsal. Without rehearsal, no one expects to put on a winning performance. Jazz ensembles are slightly different, since every performance is, in effect, 'a rehearsal' – the experimentation and creativity of rehearsal is played out in front of an audience.

Rehearsal is not the same as practise, and the two should not be confused.

Practise is about running over something many times – one small element of a dance routine; a difficult musical phrase; the lines in a play – until it is committed to memory and can be performed without thinking. Our bodies take over and deliver the physical actions, which leaves our minds free to decide, in a live performance, exactly how we want to deliver that action or phrase: its weight; its timing; its accent.

Rehearsal, on the other hand, is a process of collaborative co-creation. Everything is allowed; nothing is prohibited. One player offers something to the ensemble and it is taken up and played with, not criticized. If it doesn't lead to a successful outcome, it is dropped by common consent (or because the director, who is in charge, but not in control, decides that it should be dropped) and a new avenue is explored. The appropriate mindset is, 'yes, and...' We accept what is offered, add something of our own to it, and offer it back, until a point is reached where everyone is happy, or it is accepted that this is a blind alley. Rehearsal accepts that all ideas are 'half-baked' when they are first proposed and that the job of rehearsal is to try to fully bake the ideas. Many organizations seem to recognize that they need to foster an environment in which innovation can thrive, yet they are resistant to the very idea of 'playing around' with ideas. There is no spirit of 'yes, and...' Ideas that are not yet fully baked are shot down in flames and dismissed.

The possibility of real rehearsal also presupposes the existence of a genuine ensemble: the group of people who are involved in rehearsal must leave their egos and their social or professional status outside the door of the rehearsal room.

Next time we 'rehearse' anything – a crucial presentation, for example – it might be useful to consider whether we are really rehearsing or merely practicing. Have we got some other people in the room, and asked them to imagine that they are the audience for our presentation? Are some of the people who helped to create that presentation, in whatever way, also in the room? Is there a dialogue? When someone says, 'That's not working', do we bridle or make changes?

On a larger scale, if we are planning an organizational change, it is worth thinking about whether we have genuinely rehearsed the change, or whether we are intending simply to plan and implement it. If we intend to plan and implement, we have to accept that there will almost certainly be some nasty surprises along the way as our elegant plan bumps up against messy reality. A plan is only as clever as the people who devised it; real rehearsal taps into communal creativity and is organic – it recognizes and welcomes the fact that the best ideas may come from people who are 'minor players'.

We must also accept that planning and implementation prevents any kind of co-creation and genuine collaboration, which means both that people will not feel any sense of ownership of 'the plan', but also that we are abandoning the potential to 'think as we work' that comes with creative rehearsal. Real rehearsal also creates genuine involvement and inspiration for the people involved.

5. Do we have the right people in the room?

Many decisions are taken, in our real and our professional lives, in the absence of the people who will be influenced by that decision and of the people whose help is needed to turn that decision into reality. We focus too much on 'protagonists' and assume they are capable of acting successfully on their own. In fact, protagonists are entirely dependent on supporting roles and it is essential to have other roles 'in the room' at some point.

This is best understood in terms of the theatre: playwrights write plays featuring several characters; there will typically be some 'main' characters and several 'minor' characters. The purpose of the minor characters is to remind us of the environment in which the action takes place and to ground it in reality. No character exists in a vacuum; the minor characters exist to provide context for the actions of the protagonists. Performing the play without the minor characters results in a very different play. Much of the colour and subtlety is lost, and also most of the reality.

Modern organizations have become fixated on the protagonists, and seem to have forgotten about the existence of the essential cast of people who actually make things happen and who create the context within which the protagonists are able to act.

To make well-informed decisions, and to be sure that ideas hatched in the boardroom can be turned into reality throughout the organization, we need to involve representatives from all parts of the organization. These different voices bring different and entirely valid perspectives which must be heard, and may be revelatory. Organizations tend to take decisions in rooms where everyone is a protagonist; everyone is Hamlet. This never happens in the performing arts. No winning performance can be staged without the entire cast and crew coming together at various times, no matter what their relative roles may be. Everyone will be involved and will have their chance to comment and contribute. If we hope to put on a winning performance, we need to get the right people in the room and let them engage with each other.

6. Work on the inputs that will create the desired outputs

In business, we tend to focus almost entirely on the 'results' – the things that can be easily measured – and we lose focus on the core activities, or inputs, that are producing those results. It is perfectly possible for any project or organization to have a near-perfect set of results on all of the key metrics that are thought to reflect successful performance, but still to have unresolved problems at its heart that doom it to eventual failure. The quality of the inputs matters far more than the quality of the more obvious and apparent outputs.

One of the defining aspects of live performance is that feedback is immediate: the audience's reaction is immediate and obvious – the actors learn and adapt; the conductor can hear, immediately, whether what he or she has just done has produced the hoped-for sound from the choir or orchestra.

Organizations are less fortunate. Leaders rely on a variety of measures to tell them how the organization is performing, but these can only be an indirect measure of reality. They lack the gut-wrenching obviousness of the line that falls flat or the dance move that doesn't work. A business can, and does, experience this, on some level, in its 'theatre of action' – when an offering is warmly welcomed or coldly rejected at the interface with its audience, but organizations need to assess their state of health long before such decisive encounters in the theatre of action. The quality of our outputs is defined by the quality of our inputs. While this quality is easy to discern in merely mechanical things, it is the quality of our intangibles, in modern business, that really matters.

These intangibles are the same as those that apply to any performing ensemble: individual flair and flawless ensemble work; levels of trust, energy and commitment; creativity and rehearsal; inspiration and *esprit de corps*. To be able to assess these intangibles, the modern leader needs to have his or her finger on the pulse of the organization; to assess its physical and emotional health.

Today's successful leader is (or should be) less like an engineer, monitoring various dials, throwing levers and adjusting valves, and more like a director, choreographer or conductor, able to see the need for more discipline and effort in rehearsal; the false note that renders a performance unbelievable; the subtle change that will transform the mundane into the marvelous; the pace and rhythm of the overall performance that will deliver a wonderful experience to the audience.

Great directors do not carry clipboards and tick off the various measures that have been achieved. They work at the inputs (with the right people in the room) and build great partnerships. They occasionally nudge the team in the desired direction with confidence that the final result (over which they can have no real control) will be a winning performance.

7. Where is the art in what we do?

We may be technically brilliant, but are we aesthetically wonderful? Where is the art in what we do?

Great painters, dancers and musicians are, first and foremost, masters of their craft, and this enables them to perform in a way that lifts their work beyond excellence and turns it into something uplifting and transformational. Technical mastery is merely the starting point at which it becomes possible to develop artistry and flair. Top performances are technically near-perfect, by definition; winning performances are artistically satisfying.

Once we become masters of our craft, the door is suddenly open: we finally have the capability to become truly great; to turn our technical mastery into artistic brilliance. This is how winning performances are made.

True masters of their craft also have the capacity to improvise readily; they have the technical ability to take an idea that flashes into their minds and turn it into reality. This, obviously, is not a mechanistic process: it is not possible to plan and implement the exceptional, but with technical mastery and artistic sensibility, we can make the exceptional possible.

The great majority of our schooling and training – starting from an alarmingly early age – tends to discount the value of aesthetic judgment. We are pushed towards the technical solution. Artistic judgments are seen as pleasant but peripheral; nice but not necessary. The 'correct' solution will always have a reassuringly simple number attached to it. But all truly complex issues have a human component which precludes brute calculation. The solutions that we find to complexity depend on aesthetics: we choose the solutions that seem 'elegant', or that 'feel right'; to us. In the face of real complexity, there is no one solution; there are many possible solutions, all of which resist any simple analysis.

The good news is that we are capable of training our aesthetic sensibilities. As we realize that the world of human endeavour is not merely mechanistic and cannot be reduced to neat formulae and engineered solutions, we acknowledge that we must become artists: that success, even in business, depends not on the slide rule and the spreadsheet but on the paintbrush and the conductor's baton; that it is our uniquely human and creative input that can create a winning performance.

In life, as in business, we can begin to think like artists, looking for beautiful solutions. Beauty is not an abstract concept; beauty is what pleases our fellow human beings. Sometimes the beauty that the artist sees is not readily acknowledged – great artists, perhaps by definition, are 'ahead of their time'. The same is true of all great innovators.

The question for all of us is, increasingly: 'Are our solutions beautiful enough to succeed?'

8. Is our leadership shared, allowed and passed around?

In the case of every performing ensemble, there may well be some person who is 'in charge but not in control', but the core unit, the ensemble itself, does not have any one leader. That is not to say that the performance as a whole is leaderless – very few successful human enterprises are leaderless. But, in ensembles, the leadership is shared, allowed, and passed around. The result is a far more dynamic system than that represented by established, static models of leadership, with rigid hierarchies of command and control.

A performing artist may lead in parts of a performance, and be willingly followed, but may then follow the lead of some other player, regardless of their 'significance' in the ensemble. This shared power is exhilarating; it provides a great proportion of the joy that artists find in performance. I set out in one direction, but your idea is slightly different. As we work together, in the moment, to find the best solution, we share in the joy of creativity. We are both equal before the task of producing something new and, hopefully, wonderful. If the leader attempts to force a solution on the ensemble, this becomes like 'push-pull' in a dancing partnership: the agreed leadership of one person must be allowed, otherwise the non-leaders are being 'pushed around'. The inevitable consequence of people being pushed around is disengagement. Shared leadership, by contrast, creates engagement. The human energy that is lost when organizations attempt to impose unwelcome structures on people's behaviour is brought back into play – and enhanced – when people experience the exhilaration of shared power.

There is an interesting corollary to this approach to leadership, which is that the leader of the moment must bring their unique personality to bear on the task. Offering a lead while pretending to be someone else is simply perverse. The real meaning of 'authentic' leadership is not to offer some idealized, heroic version of oneself as leader, but to offer one's real self and to allow the other members of the ensemble to work with that. To do this, leaders must be transparent and unafraid. This ability to be unafraid and trusting is at the heart of what is involved in building a genuine ensemble.

In business, as in life, we feel the urge to control things. The world is messy and dangerous, and we feel safer when we have imposed order on it. This is not foolish, but there is a trade-off to be made. When we have complete order, we have no happy surprises; when we have complete control, there is no inspiration.

The work that results from all leadership is produced by other people. Leaders will be expert in their own field, but cannot be expert in every field. The work of the leader is to enable wonderful results from people who are more expert in their own field than the leader themselves. In this book we have seen the leader described as 'a visible boss who listens' and who focuses on what is successful and unsuccessful. What is unsuccessful is discarded without ceremony or recrimination; what is successful is taken up. These successful leaders nudge and 'bend' the performance in the desired direction. They recognize that, while they may be in a position of power, it is the organization that holds the force. In order to drive creativity and inspiration, they offer constraints rather than restraints. The key phrase is not, 'do not do this or that', but rather, 'what happens if we try it this way?'

The workers – or players – can also be trusted to take care of the details. This is what they have been trained to do. The leader who obsesses with detail cannot deliver the bigger picture.

9. Are we helping one another to perform brilliantly?

At the heart of all performance art is the interesting paradox that all performers have large egos – shrinking violets do not clamour to get onto a stage in front of an audience and invite people to judge their performance – yet all performing artists understand that their performance is completely dependent on the performance of their fellow artists. There are a few exceptions, obviously: the stand-up comedian lives or dies by himself or herself; the star soloist performs with a supporting band or orchestra with whom they have spent little time rehearsing, and it is the band's or orchestra's job to support the soloist in every twist and turn of their performance. But these examples are not representative of true ensemble performance, which is judged as a whole. Good ensemble work is collaborative, or it is nothing. Individual egos and hierarchies are subsumed to the greater good; the energy of large individual egos is harnessed to deliver the sparkling ensemble performance.

In the world of work, we are very bad at building real teams. The old, mechanistic habit of seeing everything as an individual unit drives organizations to see people separately rather than as members of various groups, preventing the creation of real partnerships and genuine ensembles.

In the context of 'helping each other to be brilliant', it is interesting to see how performing artists react to criticism. Expert criticism is taken in the spirit in which it is offered – as a chance to improve. No time is wasted in regret or denial; if the artist agrees that there is a weakness in their performance, they seize on the information and set to work. In the world of work, egos seem to be (surprisingly) more brittle. Any criticism is a personal affront, to be wrapped up in the platitudes of 'appraisals' and 'performance reviews' and 'skill enhancements'. Performing artists have large but robust egos. They very much want to win. If you can tell them something that will help them to win, they will thank you and get onto it.

10. Are we delivering a winning performance?

The performing mindset has many subtleties. At its heart is an intense focus on one's own actions and on the actions of one's fellow artists. Their actions feed your reactions; how you respond changes what they do. This constant, instantaneous interplay in the moment is key to the very concept of performance.

The other core aspect of performance is projection: the performing artist focuses on 'getting their performance across' to their audience: on telling the story; on allowing the audience to understand and be able to share in the emotions that their character is experiencing, or in successfully transmitting the ideas and emotions inherent in the music that they are playing.

Business tends to think in terms of products. If we have made a product that people want to buy, we like to believe that we have succeeded. But truly successful companies do more than create and market desirable products; they create a winning performance.

Apple, for example, has produced a remarkable series of iconic products, but the overall 'performance' that was to make Apple the world's most valuable corporation has to do with far more than technically brilliant, aesthetically wonderful products. After Steve Jobs returned as CEO to the company he co-founded, he instigated a fundamental shift in its advertising strategy. Instead of showing us products we might want to buy, Apple began to tell us about its philosophy; its reason to exist. Under the campaign headline, 'Think different', a new advertising campaign told us that Apple was on the side of the crazy guys. "Here's to the crazy ones," said the narrator, while images of Albert Einstein, Mahatma Ghandi, John Lennon, Thomas Edison, Bob Dylan, Pablo Picasso and others flickered across the screen, "... because the people who are crazy enough to think they can change the world are the ones who do."

Apple had moved from being a company that made computers and ancillary products to being an organization with a purpose; a point of view. It had always positioned its personal computers as being more 'creative'; being more intuitive to use and better suited to creative work. Now it was taking that logic further: Apple made the products that helped you to express your inner genius; using an Apple product gave you the feeling that you could be one of the 'crazy ones' and perhaps even change the world; it said something about you - you were an Apple sort of person.

When Apple launched its Apple Stores in 2001, retail analysts declared it would never be able to generate enough sales per square foot to make a profit from its beautifully presented stores in expensive locations. Worse still, sales assistants would be helpful and non-aggressive (how crazy is that?!). The analysts declared that the whole idea was a vanity project, doomed to fail.

From Apple's perspective, the driving force was to regain control of the way in which its products were presented to the consumer. It had already severed its connections with the 'big box' retailers, where Apple products were poorly presented and sales staff had no specialist training in using them. The new stores would offer expert advice, repairs and technical support; even free workshops and training on how to get the most out of Apple products. Visiting an Apple store was an exciting and glamorous occasion and made people feel good about themselves, about their product choices and about Apple. Apple stores came to generate the highest sales per unit area in the US, utterly confounding the early sceptics. The Apple stores were pure theatre, and Apple as a whole was putting on a great performance for its audience – its consumers.

Apple is a prime example of a company that has understood that the way in which we experience many products is, or has the capacity to be, far more complex than the simple act of purchase. Many modern goods no longer simply fulfil a simple need or solve a simple problem. That is the route, after all, to commoditization. Successful companies are in the business of adding value to their products; of offering not just a product but an experience; a set of values; a way of life. Successful companies do not merely sell great products and services, they put on a great performance.

There are many other examples. The American motor cycle manufacturer, Harley Davidson, not only managed to survive the Great Depression but succeeded in creating a lifestyle around its brand, with their distinctive motorcycle designs and the hugely successful Harley Owners Group, with over one million members. Owning a Harley Davidson is like buying into a slice of US history and joining a thriving community of like-minded people at the same time. For Harley Davidson's audience, it's a highly enjoyable and rewarding show.

Starbucks founder, Howard Schulz, visited a trade fair in Milan, Italy, and was struck by the way in which the city's espresso bars functioned as social hubs. He set out to create coffee shops in the US that would offer 'a third place between work and home'. Starbucks coffee houses, like Apple Stores, became places of theatre, inviting you, in this case, to settle down in a comfortable chair and while away some time over a decent cup of coffee; to feel that you were, indeed, in a home away from home. The coffee was the core ingredient, but the overall performance was what drew the crowds.

Tony Hsieh, founder of online retailer Zappos, decided that the only way to create happy customers was to have a happy call centre team. Hsieh set out to foster an atmosphere of 'fun and a little weirdness' in his call centres. There was free food and drink and even free dry-cleaning. Staff were encouraged to spend time together out of the office so they would become friends – in stark contrast to the practice of some call-centres, which deliberately stagger sales executives' coffee breaks to prevent 'time-wasting' socializing. Zappos's customers were able to return unwanted items for up to a year, postage paid. Getting a selection of shoes from Zappos through the post, trying them on, and returning the ones that weren't quite right was a fun way to shop. Dealing with the Zappos sales team was fun too. Hsieh gave sales staff a free hand to do whatever they felt was needed to make a customer happy, and put no limits on the length or content of sales calls. One sales executive set a record by talking to one customer for nine hours and 37minutes – beating the previous record of a mere eight hours and 47 minutes. They talked, as you might imagine, about a lot of things other than shoes, though a pair of Ugg boots was sold. The new record was celebrated throughout the organization.

The point of this, as Hsieh had correctly judged, was that happy customers began to recommend Zappos to their friends and neighbours, doing the company's advertising for free. The money and effort invested in ten-hour sales calls is rewarded by the audience's approval. This is a winning performance, created by an enthusiastic ensemble.

All of these companies are offering their customers a performance, not a transaction. The concept is also clearly demonstrated in the negative – by the lack of overall performance from many companies with which one deals. You may be happy with a particular service provider, but find that trying to contact them by phone involves being shunted through a badly designed automated phone system, designed to save the company money at the expense of your time and patience. You may like the car you have just bought, but be unhappy when the car manufacturer's distributor devotes many weeks to persuading you that an apparent problem is, in fact, a figment of your imagination, leading you to experience many very real breakdowns and recoveries before the car is finally replaced; you may be happy with your bank, but be less than joyful when a bank clerk seems to be trying to sell you a financial product in which you have expressed no interest while other customers stand in line behind you. It's the complete performance that matters.

[3] Mark Powell and Jonathan Gifford, *My Steam Engine Is Broken: Taking the organization from the industrial era to the Age of Ideas,* LID Publishing, London, 2014

Performing artists use many techniques in their search for a winning performance, the goal and focus of all of their efforts. They have a particular mindset, particular attitudes and a set of techniques that enable them to work with their fellow artists. It is a mindset and a set of techniques from which we can all learn, which will help us to transform our personal and our business lives.

At the heart of the performing artist's mindset are three essential things:

First, that you have to master your craft the hard way; there is no substitute for the thousands of hours of practise that are needed for you to be at the top of your own game.

Second, that you cannot deliver a winning performance on your own; you have to assist and enable your fellow artists' performance actively, because the success of your own performance depends on the success of their performance.

Finally, that the only testing ground of a performance is the audience. The goal of every performance is to reach out to the audience; to engage with them and take them on a revelatory and emotional journey; to send them away happy and wanting more. If the audience is not happy, the performance has failed and must be reworked.

The techniques and mindsets that we have explored in this book are the tools that performing artists use to enable them to be an effective part of an ensemble that is capable of delivering a winning performance.

They are available to all of us to help us to deliver our own winning performances in every aspect of our lives.